Bath

The First Town in North Carolina

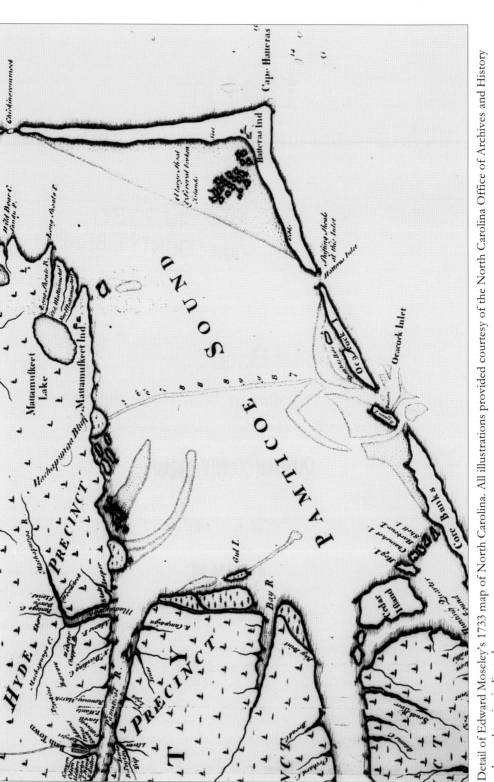

Detail of Edward Moseley's 1733 map of North Carolina. All illustrations provided courtesy of the North Carolina Office of Archives and History unless otherwise indicated.

Bath

The First Town in North Carolina

Alan Watson

with Eva C. (Bea) Latham and Patricia M. Samford

Office of Archives and History
North Carolina Department of Cultural Resources
Raleigh

In association with the Historic Bath Commission

Printed by Theo Davis Sons, Inc.

COVER: Pen and ink sketch of the Palmer-Marsh House, courtesy of Steven C. Allen and Historic Bath.

Contents

Illustrations viii

Tables ix

Preface xi

Acknowledgments xiii

1   Origins to 1715 1

2   Governance and Politics 27

3   Economy 51

4   Society 75

Epilogue: The Second and Third Centuries 109

Bibliography 133

Index 143

Illustrations

1. Detail of Edward Moseley's map of North Carolina . . . . frontispiece
2. Secotan village, by John White 3
3. Map of North and South Carolina, by John Lawson 11
4. Title page of *A New Voyage to Carolina*, by John Lawson 12
5. Site of John Lawson's lot at Bath 13
6. Edward Hyde 17
7. Von Graffenried and Lawson in captivity 20
8. Plan of Bath town lots, 1807 30
9. Sauthier's map of Bath, 1769 37
10. Customs districts in North Carolina, 1770 53
11. Colonial turpentine distillery 58
12. Reproduction of periauger 66
13. Colonial ferry 79
14. Blackbeard 81
15. Christopher Gale 83
16. Lot plan of Palmer-Marsh House and vicinity 84
17. Cellar of 1730s building near Palmer-Marsh House 85
18. Robert Palmer 88
19. The Palmer-Marsh House 91
20. Advertisement for sale of Palmer-Marsh House 92
21. George Whitefield 99
22. St. Thomas Episcopal Church (exterior) 101
23. Route of colonial post road 104
24. The Van Der Veer House 110
25. The Bonner House 111
26. Bath High School, late 1920s 116
27. Swindell's Cash Store on South Main Street 117
28. The *Marion* 119
29. Thomas R. Draper 120
30. Bath in the snow, ca. 1930 120
31. Commemorative marker, 1924 122
32. The Reverend Alexander Constantine Davis Noe 123
33. St. Thomas Episcopal Church (interior) 124
34. Edna Ferber 125
35. "Brothers of the Brush" 126
36. Governor Luther Hodges in costume 127
37. Edmund Hoyt Harding 128

Tables

Table 1   Bath Representation in the Colonial Legislature 42

Table 2   Customs Collectors for Port Bath in the Eighteenth Century . 54

Table 3   Destination of Ships Clearing Port Bath, 1768–1772 62

Table 4   Destinations of Ships Clearing Port Bath for Continental
            Colonies, 1768–1772 62

Table 5   Origin and Tonnage of Ships Entering Port Bath, 1768–1772 . 63

Table 6   Origin of Ships Entering Port Bath from Continental
            Colonies, 1768–1772 63

Table 7   Number and Tonnage of Ships Entering North Carolina
            Customs Districts, 1768–1772 67

Table 8   Number and Tonnage of Ships Clearing North Carolina
            Customs Districts, 1768–1772 67

Preface

The tercentenary of Bath, North Carolina, opens a historic window onto the state's distant colonial past. The first town to be incorporated in North Carolina (1705/6), Bath eventually was surpassed by other colonial towns such as New Bern (1710), Edenton (1722), and Wilmington (1739/40). Yet Bath played a significant role in the colony's formative years.

In 1708, a mere twelve houses and fifty people made up the town. Despite Bath's small size, political and regional factionalism, conflicts with Native Americans, and piracy placed the town at the center of the colony's stormy economic and political life. Edward Teach, also known as Blackbeard, may have lived briefly in Bath. The Anglican Church also arrived early. In 1701 St. Thomas Parish provided the colony's first public library. The oldest extant church in North Carolina (1734), St. Thomas Episcopal Church, still stands in Bath. Above all, the Pamlico River and the surrounding waterways defined Bath's place in colonial North Carolina. As the first port of entry in the colony, Bath traded raw materials such as naval stores, tobacco, and deerskins for finished products from distant shores.

Bath's riparian culture gave it one further distinction in the twentieth century. Edna Ferber, the Pulitzer-Prize-winning novelist, visited Bath in 1925. She spent time aboard the *James Adams Floating Theatre* learning the stories, legends, and lore of the waterborne theater. Her 1926 novel, *Show Boat*, became a revolutionary Broadway musical and Hollywood film because of its frank portrayal of miscegenation and racial prejudice. The musical score by Jerome Kern and Oscar Hammerstein II immortalized the story. Although hundreds of miles removed from the Mississippi River, both Bath and the Pamlico River received mention in Ferber's novel. Tiny Bath has left a sizable footprint in the state's history.

Once again the Office of Archives and History is grateful to Dr. Alan D. Watson of the University of North Carolina at Wilmington for his contribution to the historical publications program. A colonial specialist, Dr. Watson brings a thorough knowledge and insight to the history of Bath. Assisting him with this volume was Dr. Patricia Samford, manager of Historic Bath State Historic Site and section chief of the northeastern state historic sites, and Bea Latham of Historic Bath. The talented staff of the Historical Publications Section also contributed to the successful completion of the book. Special thanks go to Donna E. Kelly, section administrator, Kenrick N. Simpson, who edited the manuscript, Susan M. Trimble, who typeset it, and Lisa D. Bailey, who proofread it.

Jeffrey J. Crow
Deputy Secretary

Acknowledgments

Throughout the course of preparing this essay, the author received invaluable assistance from many individuals, all of whom contributed in various ways to the improvement of the manuscript. He wishes to thank Gerald Butler, former site manager at Historic Bath State Historic Site; Michael R. Hill, research supervisor, Office of Archives and History, and his predecessor, Jerry C. Cashion; John E. White, public services archival assistant in the Manuscripts Department of the Southern Historical Collection, University of North Carolina at Chapel Hill, and Jeanine Akers of the reference staff at Randall Library, University of North Carolina at Wilmington, for providing sources and data; and the late John H. Oden III, eminent Bath local historian, and Richard F. Knapp, historic sites specialist in the Museum and Visitor Services Section of the Division of State Historic Sites, for critiquing the manuscript. The author particularly extends his gratitude to Patricia M. Samford, present Historic Bath site manager who, with historic interpreter Eva C. (Bea) Latham and other members of her staff, carefully read and made suggestions to improve the four chapters, contributed the chapter sidebars and many of the illustrations, and substantially enlarged the epilogue.

1

Origins to 1715

Early European and English Exploration of North Carolina

As Europeans began to explore and settle the New World in the wake of the discovery by Columbus, Spain quite naturally led the way. From bases in the Caribbean Islands, Spanish vessels in the early 1520s coasted the area of North America that became North Carolina. A Spanish colonizing party led by Lucas Vasquez de Ayllon, a Spanish government official from the West Indies, may have visited the Lower Cape Fear region in 1526. Later, however, Alonso de Santa Cruz, the official Spanish cosmographer during the 1540s and 1550s, dismissed the Atlantic Coast as nothing but a group of useless islands of sand, implying not only a lack of natural resources but also a dearth of natives, both of which were essential to the sort of imperialism customarily practiced by the Spanish in the New World. Still, a reconnaissance voyage along the coast by Angel de Villafane in 1561, an accidental Spanish landing at Currituck Inlet in 1566, and a short-lived Jesuit mission in the Chesapeake region in 1570-1571 evidenced at least passing Spanish concern with the vicinity of North Carolina.[1]

Despite early Spanish interest, Giovanni da Verazzano, an Italian navigator sailing for France in 1524, was the first European to sight and leave a written account of present North Carolina. Blown off course in a rough Atlantic crossing, Verazzano made landfall at or near Cape Fear. After sailing south for about fifty leagues, he turned north to avoid a possible encounter with the Spanish. Dropping anchor first along the Cape Fear coast and treating with the natives, Verazzano then made his way north to the Outer Banks, where he extolled the flora and fauna of the region. Verazzano called one spot, perhaps present Kitty

Hawk, Arcadia, a reference to the ancient Grecian concept of an idyllic landscape inhabited by simple, virtuous people (and a term subsequently applied by mapmakers to the Canadian Maritimes and Maine). In the process he left the erroneous impression that North Carolina's sounds might offer an immediate link to the Pacific Ocean, in effect providing a water passage to the Orient that had eluded Columbus. Without attempting to verify his observation, Verazzano sailed north past present New York and Newfoundland and back to France.[2]

After the French shifted their exploration to the northern reaches of the continent, the English in the late sixteenth century assumed an interest in present North Carolina. Elizabethan courtier Walter Raleigh secured a patent from Queen Elizabeth I in 1584 to plant a colony along the southern Atlantic coast. In that year Raleigh dispatched a reconnaissance expedition commanded by Philip Amadas and Arthur Barlowe to the New World to seek an appropriate location for a settlement. Like Verazzano, Amadas and Barlowe were captivated by the Outer Banks, resplendent in verdant undergrowth and trees at that time. Perhaps influenced by the accolades showered upon the Carolina coast by Verazzano as well as his erroneous belief that North Carolina coastal waters offered ready access to the Pacific Ocean, and reinforced in his sentiments by the reports of Amadas and Barlowe, Raleigh determined to site his colony near the Outer Banks.[3]

The intent of the Roanoke Island expedition of 1585, led by Sir Richard Grenville and governed by Ralph Lane, appeared to be the establishment of a military base designed to support forays against Spanish possessions in America. Although the colony never served its intended purpose, Grenville, Lane, and John White, artist and future governor of the second Roanoke Island settlement known as the "Lost Colony," explored extensively the sound region of North Carolina, including present Pamlico Sound and Beaufort County. In the process the English found that the region had long been inhabited by Native Americans of the Algonquian linguistic group, the Secotan and Pomoik or Pamlico. These were among the southernmost of a number of Algonquian tribes, including the Powhatans in Virginia, that extended north along the Atlantic coast to Canada, where they were far more numerous and powerful, and provided allies for the French in the contest against the English for control of North America. John White's 1585 map labels the area "Seco," while early-seventeenth-century maps show a village in the vicinity of Bath named, variously, Cotan and Secotan.[4]

The Secotan and Pamlico occupied the area between the Albemarle and Pamlico Sounds. The former lived along the banks of the Pamlico River; the latter, to the south and west of the Secotan territory. Hence the Secotan probably constituted the subjects of John White's magnificent drawings and watercolors. Open warfare between the Secotan and Pamlico, characteristic of a bitter,

Watercolor of Secotan village by John White.

long-standing rivalry, had been concluded by a truce in the early 1580s, just before the arrival of the English, though both tribes remained acutely suspicious of one another. Historian David Beers Quinn has theorized that the probable location of the Indian town Secotan, depicted on late-sixteenth-century maps drawn by the Roanoke Island colonists, lay near the northern bank of the Pamlico River, at or not far from the future town of Bath. However, conclusive proof of the site of Secotan has failed to surface, and ambiguity over the use of names of tribes as opposed to towns further obscures the question. Moreover, the future site of the town of Bath lay along the border of the regions claimed by the Secotan and Pamlico. A Native American settlement in the vicinity of Bath could have represented the presence of either tribe.[5]

After the failure of the Elizabethan attempts to colonize Roanoke Island, Sir Robert Heath of England obtained a grant in 1629 from King Charles I for an area called Carolana, which included present North and South Carolina. Although Heath and his assignees were never able to mount a permanent settlement in present North Carolina, Virginians showed an interest in the territory. Explorations, military expeditions against Indians, and fur-trading activities brought many Virginians into contact with North Carolina by the mid-seventeenth century. Some obtained grants to land along the Roanoke and Chowan Rivers from the Virginia government that claimed the area south to the Albemarle Sound. Between 1649 and 1651 four promotional tracts appeared in England lauding the Carolinas and the potential there for settlers. But it was Virginians who finally moved into North Carolina permanently in the late 1650s, buying land from the Indians, and establishing settlements west of the Pasquotank River, at the head of Currituck Sound, and west of the Chowan River. In effect, they extended the southern frontier of Virginia, but to their dismay the Virginians soon found themselves separated from their parent colony.[6]

The Lords Proprietors of Carolina

Since Heath and his assignees had never settled Carolana, King Charles II of England re-granted the land in 1663 as Carolina to eight prominent Englishmen known as the Lords Proprietors of Carolina. The area was formally divided in 1712 into North and South Carolina. As a result the Virginia settlers north of the Albemarle Sound found themselves in Carolina after 1663. Subsequent to a change in the Carolina charter by the Crown in 1665 and the imposition of two governance documents by the proprietors in 1663 and 1665, the proprietors organized the Carolina settlement into Albemarle County. Meanwhile, an attempt between 1664 and 1667 by Barbadians and New Englanders to establish a settlement along the Cape Fear River had failed. Afterwards, the proprietors devoted most of their attention to the future colony of South Carolina, started in

1670. Confounded by proprietary inattention, internal dissension, Virginia opposition to North Carolina tobacco exports, and geographic isolation, the Albemarle County settlement grew slowly.[7]

By the 1680s, as prime lands in the Albemarle had been absorbed, explorers, fur traders, and land speculators began to evidence an interest in the area south of Albemarle Sound. Seth Sothel, proprietor and controversial governor of Albemarle County (1678-1679, 1682-1689), anticipated the future prospects of the region, when in 1684 he issued to himself a land grant of twelve thousand acres on the north bank of the Pamlico River that included the site of the present town of Bath. Settlers drifted into the Pamlico area during the 1690s. For the "Incouragement of settling those parts w[hi]ch lye north of Cape Fear," the proprietors in 1694 authorized Deputy Governor John Archdale to sell land at a moderate price, though accompanied by a quitrent or land tax of not less than a halfpenny per acre.[8]

When the Carolinians moved into the Pamlico region in the last years of the seventeenth century, the Secotan Indians had disappeared, leaving the area to the Pamlico Indians, whose town (Pamtecough or Pamticoe) may have been located at or near the future site of Bath as late as the 1680s. Before 1696, however, the Pamlico had been decimated by epidemic disease, perhaps smallpox, leaving only a single settlement called "island," possibly present Indian Island, located in the Pamlico River ten miles below Bath. The settlement contained approximately fifty to seventy-five inhabitants. Still, the possibility that Bath had once been the site of a Native American settlement intrigued archaeologists in the last half of the twentieth century. William G. Haag in the 1950s tentatively concluded that Aborigines occupied Handy's Point at the juncture of Bath (originally Old Town) Creek and Back (originally Adams) Creek before 1500, a settlement that persisted into the seventeenth century. Bennie C. Keel in 1964-1965 offered support for the "presumptive site." But a thorough archaeological investigation by John L. Mattson under the supervision of Joffre L. Coe in 1968 dismissed Haag's conclusion, claiming that identification of Handy's Point as a Secotan or Pamlico site was "impossible."[9] The Native American materials recovered there dated not later than the fifteenth century.

The Formation of Beaufort County and Bath

The population below the Albemarle Sound had grown sufficiently by 1696 to justify the creation of Bath County, honoring John Granville, Earl of Bath, one of the Lords Proprietors. Nine years later, in 1705, Bath County was divided into three precincts, Pamptecough, Wickham, and Archdale, which in 1712 were renamed Beaufort, Hyde, and Craven, to honor three of the proprietors of

Bath on the Eve of Incorporation

At the end of the seventeenth century, the Lords Proprietors anxiously sought to promote settlement in northeastern North Carolina by establishing towns to serve as centers of trade and government. Developing urban centers proved difficult, however, and the predominantly rural nature of the area still persists. At the turn of the eighteenth century, a traveler through the countryside around the future site of Bath encountered largely wilderness—vast stretches of pine and hardwood forests, interrupted only by creeks and wetlands. Punctuating this wilderness were isolated plantations, located along the broad creeks that served as the main arteries of travel, communication, and trade in what was then known as Bath County.

Given the isolated nature of settlement, each plantation was largely self-sustaining. Such self-reliance necessitated the construction of buildings to shelter people and animals, and structures in which to store and process crops and foodstuffs. On the tracts of wealthier landowners, the assortment of outbuildings included kitchens, smokehouses, stables, dairies, privies, and laborers' quarters. Often these isolated plantations presented the appearance of small villages to travelers. Fenced enclosures—to keep livestock out of the yards and kitchen gardens—were typical during this period. William Brice in 1701 purchased the Old Town (Bath) Creek plantation that included a house, an established nursery, and an orchard of apple and cherry trees. Crops grown on these plantations included tobacco, wheat, and corn.

Recent archaeological excavations at an early-eighteenth-century plantation in Bertie County provide clues about the appearance of early Bath plantations. Wood was the most commonly used construction material, and many of the early buildings were supported with a frame of upright posts sunken in the ground. By today's standards, homes—even of the wealthy—were small and the rooms multi-functional. The homes of poor to middling farmers often had chimneys constructed of sticks and mud

Carolina. At that time Beaufort Precinct, described as "Lying on the north side of Pamptecough River and beginning at Molines's Creek, and westerly to the head of the river," contained all or part of the future counties of Pitt, Martin, and Pamlico.[10] Beaufort Precinct became Beaufort County in 1739, when the General Assembly of North Carolina eliminated the large counties of Albemarle and Bath, and transformed all the precincts into counties.

instead of brick, and windows protected from the elements by wooden shutters rather than glass. Wealthier planters could generally afford to finish the interior walls of their homes with plaster. Early Bath area resident William Barrow hired brick mason William Tomson to plaster his home in 1701 or 1702.

The east and west sides of Old Town Creek were settled by the late seventeenth century. Large tracts of property—such as the 640 acres obtained by Capt. Thomas Nicholas Jones at the mouth of Bath Creek in 1700—were representative of many of the early plantations. Such sizable homesteads would have been ideal for pioneer settlers who utilized the extensive pine forests for naval stores to complement their crops and livestock. Many of the recorded court transactions prior to 1705 occurred at the homes of William Barrow and James Nevill. Barrow lived north of the future site of Bath, and Nevill probably resided near the mouth of Blount's Creek on the Pamlico River. Other early owners of plantations on the east and west shores of Old Town Creek included Simon Alderson, Joel Martin, John Lawson, Collingwood Ward, Francis Garganus, and William Brice.

Property changed hands often, suggesting that many tracts remained undeveloped in the early years of the eighteenth century and may have been purchased speculatively. While money was in short supply, land was virtually limitless and essentially served as "coin of the realm." Colonists used land to pay off debts and to satisfy other obligations.

Although isolation encouraged self-sufficiency, early residents did have access to a store operated by Col. Robert Quary. A former governor of the South Carolina colony and future surveyor general for North Carolina, Quary apparently arrived in Bath around the turn of the century. By 1700, he had opened a mercantile establishment southeast of the present site of Bath, between Back Creek and Romney Marsh. Stores formed an important part of the colonial economy. There, residents traded their crops, naval stores, and other wood products for a wide variety of goods shipped from England and the Caribbean.

Settlement in Bath County concentrated along the Pamlico River and its tributaries, including Bath Creek, where John Lawson, Joel Martin, Simon Alderson, David Perkins, William Barrow, William Brice, Levi Truewhite, David Depee, Richard Collins, Robert Daniel, John Burras, and Collingwood Ward, among others, owned plantations in the early eighteenth century. They were joined about 1704 or 1705 by a group of French Protestants, or Huguenots, who had emigrated from the settlement called Manakin Town (Manokin, Mannakintown) on the James River in Virginia. A thrifty, industrious, cosmopolitan people, the Huguenots mingled easily with the English populace. Some eventually left the Pamlico for the Neuse-Trent area and New Bern; others remained to help settle Bath, as later recognized by a Beaufort Precinct deed that mentioned the "house the French people lived in."[11]

At the time of the creation of Pamptecough Precinct, a half century after the permanent settlement of North Carolina, the colony had yet to produce a town. Urbanization made little impress upon the English provinces along the North American coast before the Revolution. Only Philadelphia, New York, Boston, Newport, Rhode Island, and the South Carolina capital of Charleston (originally Charles Town) had achieved a population of ten thousand by the time of independence. Still, of the thirteen colonies, North Carolina was one of the most rural, and one of the few not settled about a town. From Jamestown, Charleston, and Savannah in the South, to Plymouth, Providence, New Haven, and New York in the North, most English provinces radiated from urban origins. North Carolina, on the other hand, simply appeared as an extension of Virginia. Much like Virginians, settlers in the Albemarle had little need of towns, scattered as they were along the sounds, rivers, and streams, which served well as arteries of immigration and trade.

The Lords Proprietors of Carolina realized immediately the need for towns in the colony to act as centers of commerce, defense, and culture. The Carolina Charter of 1663 empowered the proprietors to "Erect, raise, and build, within the ... Province ... so many Forts, Fortresses, Castles, Cities, Boroughs, Towns, Villages, and other Fortifications ... as shall be thought fit and convenient." In turn the proprietors in the Concessions and Agreement of 1665, a document outlining the governance of the colony, authorized the General Assembly or legislature to establish "Forts, ... Cities, Boroughs, towns, Villages and other places of strength and defence." Later, in the Fundamental Constitutions of 1669, which attempted to impose upon Carolina a systematic, orderly settlement reflecting English society, the proprietors provided for the erection of towns to be governed by a mayor, aldermen, and a council. In that year the General Assembly in the Albemarle tried to encourage the formation of towns when it prohibited "Adventurers" from importing and "engrossing" commodities for retail at exorbitant prices unless such persons "shall keep Shoppe or retaile any sort of comodytys in any Towne that is or shall be erected by the Lords Proprietors or by their order."[12]

Carolinians in the Albemarle remained unmoved. As early as 1665, one reported to the proprietors that "to reduce Planters into Townes, is here almost impossible." Three-quarters of a century later Gov. Gabriel Johnston agreed, observing that the "people both here and in Virginia are very far from being fond of Towns." Although the settlement begun in 1664 along the banks of the Cape Fear River included a town, Charles Town, located at the junction of the river and Town Creek, the colony was abandoned in 1667. Undaunted, the proprietors in 1676 ordered the erection of three port towns in northern North Carolina, a "chiefe town" on Roanoke Island and others on the west bank of Little River in Perquimans Precinct. According to the proprietors, "wee must assure you that it is your and our Concerne very much to have some very good Towns in your Plantations for other wise you will not longe continue civillized or ever bee considerable or secure."[13]

Urbanization of a sort finally reached North Carolina when the General Assembly on March 8, 1705/6, incorporated Bath Town. The settlement had been under development for several months, perhaps a year or more, before its incorporation. Over the years the early grant to Seth Sothel had been ignored or vacated, for David Perkins had subsequently obtained title to the land on which Bath was situated. Perkins in turn sold sixty acres of his tract to John Lawson, Joel Martin, and Simon Alderson, probably in 1704 or 1705, for the creation of a town. Even before incorporation the town had been named Bath and surveyed, and several lots sold or assigned, for on February 11, 1705/6, Alderson conveyed a lot in "Bath Town formerly called Jacob Conrow's Lott" to Nathaniel Wyersdale. A grant to Perkins on March 2, 1705/6, doubtlessly was a re-grant of the property earlier acquired by Perkins and meant to confirm the sale of his sixty acres to Lawson, Martin, and Alderson, because six days later the legislature incorporated Bath.[14]

John Lawson and the Founding of Bath

John Lawson, a remarkable Englishman who contributed greatly to the development of early North Carolina, probably spearheaded the effort to establish Bath. Having lived in London and being well educated in the natural sciences, Lawson embarked for America in 1700 after the Lords Proprietors appointed him to make a reconnaissance survey of the interior of Carolina. In December Lawson began a fifty-five-day, approximately 550-mile tour of present South Carolina and North Carolina that took him from Charleston northwest to present Camden, South Carolina, and then north into North Carolina in the vicinity of present Charlotte and High Point. At that juncture, he traveled eastward past present Durham and Greenville to the English settlements along the Pamlico River, where in late February 1701, "being well receiv'd by the Inhabitants, and pleas'd with the Goodness of the Country, we all resolv'd to continue."[15]

Lawson remained in North Carolina until his untimely death in 1711 at the hands of the Tuscarora Indians. He first built a house near the confluence of the Neuse and Trent Rivers, the future site of New Bern, and later surveyed and helped to settle that town in 1710. Meanwhile, Lawson served as the deputy of Edward Moseley, surveyor general of North Carolina, and may have succeeded Moseley in that capacity. From 1707 to 1708 Lawson held the positions of clerk of court and public register for Pamptecough Precinct. He also acquired land and appears to have been a moderately successfully planter and fur trader as well as public official. While in England in 1709, Lawson secured an appointment from the Lords Proprietors as one of the commissioners for North Carolina to survey the boundary between that colony and Virginia. The attempt to run the boundary in 1710 failed, but at the time Lawson must have considered the line a demarcation. When the boundary was ultimately surveyed in 1728, the line deviated only "half a minute . . . [from] the observation made formerly by Mr. Lawson, . . . w[hi]ch was but a small difference," according to Virginians who participated in the survey.[16]

Lawson journeyed to England in 1708 to promote the publication of *A New Voyage to Carolina*, essentially a compendium of the journal of his earlier travel through Carolina and his subsequently accumulated information about the Pamlico-Neuse region. In addition to the journal account of his travels, Lawson provided separate sections on the geography, flora, fauna, crops and vegetables, Europeans, and Native Americans of Carolina, including a lengthy list of words in several Indian dialects. The volume was rushed into print in 1709 and proved so popular that it was reissued several times during the next decade, along with German editions in 1709 and 1722, probably to encourage German immigration to America. Moreover, several authors, including John Brickell and William Byrd, subsequently attested to the compelling importance of Lawson's work by plagiarizing parts of it. A reading of *A New Voyage to Carolina* is indispensable for a proper understanding of early-eighteenth-century North Carolina at the time of the founding of Bath. The volume remains today, in the estimation of one historian, "the one significant contribution of a North Carolinian to the literature of colonial America."[17]

Perhaps the most remarkable feature of *A New Voyage to Carolina* was Lawson's appreciation for Native Americans and their relationship with the Europeans. The book reinforced the then current western European construct of the "Noble Savage," the idea of a "free and wild being who draws directly from nature virtues which raise doubts as to the value of civilization." Lawson joined that small minority who dissented from the view that Native Americans were barbarous heathens who blocked the path of civilization and settlement, and thus became candidates for eradication. From their disregard for wealth and their

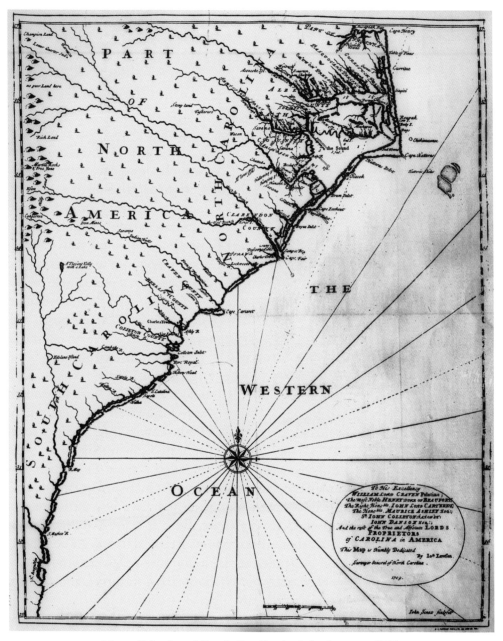

Map of North and South Carolina by John Lawson, 1709.

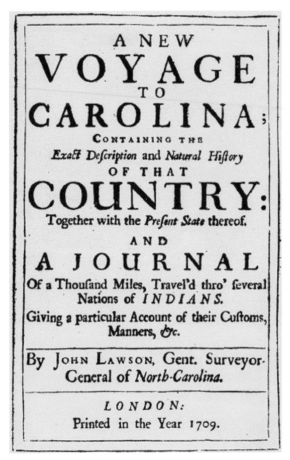

A NEW
VOYAGE
TO
CAROLINA;
CONTAINING THE
Exact Defcription and *Natural Hiftory*
OF THAT
COUNTRY:
Together with the *Prefent State* thereof.
AND
A JOURNAL
Of a Thoufand Miles, Travel'd thro' feveral
Nations of *INDIANS.*

Giving a particular Account of their Cuftoms,
Manners, &c.

By JOHN LAWSON, Gent. Surveyor-
General of *North-Carolina.*

LONDON:
Printed in the Year 1709.

Title page of John Lawson's *A New Voyage to Carolina*, 1709.

carefree life to their hospitality and physique, Lawson favorably compared Indians to whites. Setting Lawson apart from other proponents of the Noble Savage, however, was his advocacy of the union of the natives and Europeans as a prerequisite for the civilization and Christianization of the Indian. He proposed that governments subsidize interracial marriages for that purpose.[18]

Lawson may well have selected the site for Bath, which was located at the junction of Bath Creek and Back Creek, about 1.25 miles from the Pamlico River. Thus Bath was well sheltered but commanded the traffic of two creeks and the river, and offered the potential for developing into a port. Moreover, the town was situated about fifty-five miles by water from Ocracoke Inlet, the best ingress and egress for shipping along the North Carolina coast above Beaufort Inlet. Although no longer extant, the legislation incorporating Bath doubtlessly directed the town's commissioners, Lawson, Joel Martin, and Nicholas Daw, to survey and sell lots, and to enforce other provisions of the law.[19]

Bath grew slowly during its formative years. The earliest surviving record of sale of property in the town after its incorporation occurred on September 27, 1706, when the commissioners sold thirteen lots. Before the end of October at least twenty-five individuals had purchased lots. Among the early property owners were Lawson, Alderson, Martin, Perkins, Carrow (Conrow), Giles Shute, and Nathaniel Wyersdale as well as Huguenots Dr. Maurice Luellyn and Mons. Perdree and Jadrian. However, lots in Bath changed hands often, an indication of speculation as opposed to permanent residency. According to

Excavation of the site of John Lawson's lot in Bath. Photo courtesy of Dr. Charles Ewen, Department of Anthropology, East Carolina University.

Anglican missionary William Gordon in 1709, Bath "consists of about twelve houses. . . . I must own, it is not the unpleasantest part of the country, nay, in all probability it will be the centre of trade." But two years later, the Reverend John Urmstone, another Anglican missionary and inveterate critic of North Carolina and its people, found Bath "the most obscure inconsiderable place in the country."[20]

John Lawson, who continued to maintain a residence in the vicinity of the Neuse River, quite naturally numbered among the first inhabitants of Bath. No doubt having his choice of property, he selected lots 5 and 6 at the corner of Main (formerly Water, Bay) and Front Streets on which the Bonner House later stood, and a site that commands a view of the junction of Bath and Back Creeks. By December 1706, Lawson had built a house accompanied by outbuildings and probably a wharf or landing, all of which he leased to Hannah Smith, his wife or mistress. She was probably the daughter of Richard Smith, a plantation owner along the Pamlico River whom Lawson had met when he first entered North Carolina. At his death in 1711 Lawson left his house and lots to his "Dearly beloved Hannah Smith" for her lifetime, together with one-third of his personal estate. The remainder of his property was bequeathed in equal shares to Isabella Lawson, his daughter, and the unborn child or children with whom Hannah Smith was pregnant.[21]

Despite a small population Bath soon became a bustling business community. Ships dropped anchor in Bath Creek in front of Main (Water) Street, bringing manufactured goods from northern colonies and seeking cargoes of country produce that included furs and deerskins, naval stores, and various wood products. Merchants, including George Birkenhead, often maintained stores in their homes. John Jordan, a cooper, represented the artisans in town as did ship carpenter Thomas Harding, who agreed to build a sloop for Thomas Cary at the latter's landing in Bath. Lawson, Luellyn, and Christopher Gale erected a gristmill on Gale's property fronting Bath Creek at which they ground their own corn and that of others for a fee.[22]

Adding excitement to the town were meetings of the Bath County Court of Pleas and Quarter Sessions, which served Craven and Hyde as well as Beaufort Precinct. The court convened in Bath as early as October 1706. However, the many visitors to the town during court days overwhelmed the facilities of the tavern keepers, which "have not beads (beds) to Lodge us in which constrains us either to be burthinsum to ye gentel-men in town or Else to lay by ye fire side . . . which [would be a] great Hardship."[23]

Cary's Rebellion

Soon after the founding of Bath, inhabitants of the town became embroiled in a colony-wide dispute called Cary's Rebellion, one of a long train of political controversies that wracked early North Carolina. From the outset turbulence and tumult marked the colony, largely inspired by the tension between the older or preproprietary settlers from Virginia and those who arrived after 1663 and represented the interests of the proprietors. Unrest in the mid-1670s culminated in Culpeper's Rebellion in 1677, a confusing incident that stemmed not only from political antagonisms but also from the lack of a duly constituted government in the Albemarle region. Subsequently Gov. Seth Sothel was banished from the province in 1689 for arbitrary imprisonments and illegal confiscation of property. The following year Gibbs's Rebellion found John Gibbs and Philip Ludwell contesting the governorship of the Albemarle. After the Lords Proprietors settled that matter, North Carolina enjoyed the leadership of able executives for a decade and a half, during which time the colony expanded its bounds into the Pamlico region and Bath was founded.[24]

Cary's Rebellion originated in the opposition of Quakers to their disbarment from public office but ultimately represented a power struggle between Albemarle and Bath Counties. Members of the Society of Friends constituted the first element of organized religion in North Carolina and exercised considerable influence in the colony's government, particularly after Quaker John Archdale became deputy governor in 1694. But five years later Henderson Walker, a zealous Anglican, replaced Archdale, and early in the eighteenth century the General Assembly passed legislation to establish the Church of England as the colony's official church. Subsequently Deputy Governor Robert Daniel refused to accept the Quaker affirmation as a substitute for an oath, in effect preventing Quakers from holding government office. The Quakers protested to the proprietors and secured the appointment of South Carolina merchant Thomas Cary as deputy governor from whom they expected more lenient treatment.[25]

Cary, however, aligned himself with the Anglicans, led by Thomas Pollock of Chowan Precinct, during his stint as governor from 1705 to October 1707. Again the Quakers complained to the proprietors, sending John Porter to England to denounce Cary as "an unscrupulous politician, always seeking his own advancement." The proprietors suspended all laws regarding oaths and ordered the removal of Cary. When Porter returned to North Carolina, he found Cary had gone back to South Carolina, and that William Glover as president of the council was the acting governor. Yet Glover refused to comply with the directives of the proprietors. So the Quakers negotiated with Cary to return to North Carolina to replace Glover. Cary reappeared in 1708, agreed to support the Quaker position, and was elected president of the council, in effect acting governor of the colony. After protests by Glover, both men agreed to submit their claims to the people by calling for elections for a General Assembly. Despite objections from Glover, Cary appeared victorious, receiving the support of a majority of the legislators, and assumed the governorship of the colony as president of the council. Glover, together with Cary's former ally, Thomas Pollock, apparently feared retribution from Cary and fled to Virginia.

Cary's Rebellion ultimately centered on Bath. Cary was an original lot holder in the town and owned a plantation adjacent to Bath. Superficially, the contest appeared to pit Quakers or dissenters against Anglicans. Yet the Quakers, though numerous and vocal, were confined almost altogether to the Albemarle region, where most of Cary's opposition resided. Although supported by the Quakers and solicitous of their demands, Cary and his principal followers lived in Bath County. According to historian C. Wingate Reed, when Gov. Alexander Spotswood of Virginia later issued a proclamation calling for the arrest of fugitives from Cary's Rebellion who had fled to Virginia, the list of names read "like a 'Who's Who' for Bath Town." Included were John Porter, Emanuell Low, Nevil Low, Edmund Porter, William Barrow, Thomas Sparrow, George Birkenhead, Henry Warren, Simon Alderson Jr., Samuel Boutwell, and Levi Truewhite.[26]

Underlying tensions between Albemarle and Bath Counties largely accounted for the dispute and the resort to arms that followed, leaving religion as a sidebar to Cary's Rebellion. Residents of Bath County resented the disparity of representation in the General Assembly in which each precinct in Albemarle County was entitled to five delegates in the lower house as opposed to only two delegates for each precinct in Bath County. Not only did the Albemarle control the General Assembly by virtue of the voting majority of its precincts but that area also resisted expansion and attempted to dominate the Indian fur trade that lay at the heart of the Bath County economy. In effect, Cary represented the infusion of talented, ambitious young men in Bath County who wanted political and economic recognition commensurate with their numbers and interests.

As president of the council, Cary governed the colony without incident from 1708 until January 1711, when Edward Hyde, a new executive, appeared. The proprietors in 1710 appointed Hyde, relative of a deceased proprietor and reputed cousin of Queen Anne I, as deputy governor of North Carolina. Hyde left England for the colony without his commission. However, upon arriving in North Carolina, he convinced both the Cary and Glover factions of the legitimacy of his position. Facing the loss of support by his allies, Cary surrendered the government to Hyde, who made his home in the Albemarle only a few miles from Thomas Pollock, a Chowan Precinct planter who clearly aligned himself with Cary's opposition. The Hyde faction controlled the General Assembly that met in March 1711 and proceeded to indict Cary for "High Crimes and Misdemeanors," which included a charge of inciting the Indians against friends of Hyde. After Cary was tried in absentia and found guilty, the council issued a proclamation ordering his arrest. The General Assembly also voided the proceedings of the legislature for the past two years, accused Edward Moseley, one of Cary's adherents, of embezzling public moneys and falsifying surveys as surveyor general of the province, and made it a criminal offense to "speak seditious words, write or dispense scurrilous Libels against the present Government, . . . instigate others to seditious Caball, or meet together to incite Rebellion."

From his stronghold in Bath, Cary then resorted to military measures that drove him into open rebellion against the government. Declaring that Hyde had not been duly appointed as governor and that the legislature had not been lawfully elected, Cary began to assemble an armed force with the intention of overthrowing Hyde. He obtained cannon, small arms, and powder from a ship that had recently arrived in Bath and was captained by one Roach, a friend of former governor Archdale and a supporter of Cary. Hyde responded by gathering approximately 150 men to capture Cary. Learning of Hyde's action, Cary left his home near Bath and moved to the house of Robert Daniel on Bath Creek, where he entrenched himself with forty armed men and five cannon. Hyde found Cary unwilling to accept terms of surrender and his position too well fortified to assault. After waiting futilely for Cary to change his mind, and "reluctant to bring bloodshed to the province," Hyde withdrew to the Albemarle. During the confrontation one man, a relative of Hyde, was accidentally killed.

Encouraged by Hyde's retreat, Cary and his followers counterattacked. Using Emanuell Low's brigantine, which was mounted with six cannon, and smaller vessels, they sailed to the home of Pollock on the Chowan River where Hyde and his council were meeting. Hyde with two cannon and sixty men appeared overmatched, but a lucky shot broke one of the masts on Cary's brigantine and frightened his men, who sailed away in confusion. Hyde

Edward Hyde, governor of the colony of North Carolina (1711-1712).

pursued in a sloop and found the brigantine grounded. Cary and most of his men fled on foot back to their homes. But Cary, with the help of Roach, fortified an island in the Pamlico River, gathered another armed force, and repulsed an attack by Hyde's men. Hyde then sought the aid of Virginia governor Alexander Spotswood, who sent a detachment of royal marines from a British man-of-war to the Pamlico area. Unwilling to confront the marines and risk a charge of treason, the Cary resistance collapsed. Subsequently Cary and several of his men made their way to Virginia, whereupon Spotswood ordered the arrest of Cary and "other Seditious and Fractious persons that have made their escape from North Carolina into this colony."

Upon apprehension Cary and four others were sent to England to face the proprietors. The proceedings in England continued intermittently for over a year. After the Privy Council complained about the lengthy detention, the proprietors freed all five without prescribing any punishment. The proprietors may have felt that Cary and his men, separated from North Carolina and their families for fourteen months, had suffered sufficiently, or that the confused situation in the colony from 1707 to 1711 warranted leniency. Perhaps, too, the proprietors worried that their control over North Carolina might seem so tenuous in the estimation of the Crown as to warrant a revocation of their charter. Moreover, no representative of the Hyde faction ever appeared to testify against the rebels, while John Porter had voluntarily sailed to England to present the case of Cary. In any event, the proprietors ordered that no charges be brought against Cary in North Carolina until an investigation (which was never undertaken) was made by former Virginia governor Francis Nicholson, who had already been directed by the Crown to consider a number of disorders in the colonies. Cary returned to North Carolina in the spring of 1713, and though there was apprehension that he might instigate another uprising against the government, he lived quietly, dying probably at his home on Back Creek between 1716 and 1722.

Although the North Carolina government eventually accepted Quaker affirmations in lieu of oaths, and Governor Hyde in 1712 pardoned all the rebels except Cary, Emanuell Low, John and Edmund Porter, and William Tillett, Bath County suffered during the course of the rebellion. Courts closed and government in general ceased to function in 1711 in the Pamlico region. Plundering and destruction ruined many, particularly the less fortunate. According to one observer, widespread were "the complaints of the poor men & families, who have been so long in arms that they have lost their crops & will want bread."[27] Compounding the political turmoil was a severe drought in the summer of 1711 and a yellow fever epidemic in 1711 and 1712, which occasioned the death of Governor Hyde. Worse, the disruption left Bath County vulnerable to a wholesale attack by natives.

The Tuscarora War

Within two months of the defeat of Cary's rebels, North Carolina faced an even more trying crisis—the Tuscarora War. At the time of the permanent settlement of North Carolina in the 1650s, the Iroquoian-speaking Tuscarora represented the most numerous and powerful of the Native Americans in the eastern region of the colony. Lawson in 1709 claimed that the Tuscarora had twelve hundred fighting men, a formidable force, and he probably underestimated the Indian population since he omitted reference to several Tuscarora towns now known to have existed at that time. Separated from the ocean by small Algonquian tribes, including the Pamlico, Core, Bay or Bear River, Hatteras, Machapunga, and Neusioc, the Tuscarora dominated their weaker neighbors, treating them as tributary tribes, which increased the overall strength of the Tuscarora. At the same time the Tuscarora were aligned with the Five (Iroquoian) Nations below the Great Lakes in the area of present New York and connected to tribes in the Piedmont, Mountain region, and beyond, perhaps as far as the Mississippi River. So powerful were the Tuscarora that in fact they acted as a barrier to white expansion in North Carolina for a half century.[28]

However, whites continually challenged the hegemony of the Tuscarora and their allies as they tentatively made their way down the coast, across Albemarle Sound by 1690, and into the Neuse-Trent and Onslow regions by 1700. In the meantime whites further antagonized the natives, systematically cheating them in trade relations, often through the liberal use of alcohol, and enslaving the Indians. Complaints by whites in 1703 and 1704 against the Pamlico, Core, Bear, Hatteras, Neusioc, and others evidenced the restiveness among the Indians, and the Tuscarora availed themselves of the dissatisfaction by forming alliances with the smaller tribes. Fur traders in Virginia were rumored to have encouraged the Tuscarora to attack the whites along the Pamlico and Neuse as a way to eliminate competition. The Tuscarora may also have been pressured or encouraged to take action in North Carolina by the Five Nations to the north, who were embroiled in the conflict between the French and the English (Queen Anne's War). The catalyst for the outbreak of the war in North Carolina in 1711, however, may well have been the establishment in 1710 of a town south of Bath at the confluence of the Neuse and Trent Rivers—New Bern.

At dawn on September 22, 1711, the Tuscarora under the leadership of Chief Hancock, together with Indians from the Core, Pamlico, Machapunga, and Bear tribes, launched a coordinated attack on white settlements along the Pamlico and Neuse Rivers. Hancock probably sought a quick strike at outlying homes in hopes of curtailing white expansion and reestablishing a buffer between the Tuscarora and the Carolina settlers. Fortunately for the whites the northern Tuscarora under Chief Tom Blount decided not to join those of the Pamlico region, for the future of North Carolina would have been jeopardized. As it stood, the southern Tuscarora wreaked devastation in Bath County, killing 150 settlers at the outset, driving off or killing livestock, burning houses, and destroying crops. John Lawson was an early casualty. About a week before the attack, Lawson and Baron Christoph von Graffenried, founder of New Bern, were captured in the vicinity of New Bern and taken to Catechna or Hancock's Fort near present Snow Hill, the center of the conspiracy. While sparing Graffenried, who promised the neutrality of New Bern, the Indians executed Lawson, probably by torture, never appreciating the irony that they had killed perhaps their most sympathetic and valuable ally among the whites.

Carolinians in the Pamlico and Neuse area left their farms to gather in a few defensible locations, principally Bath, which apparently escaped the devastation of the opening attack, though the house belonging to John Lillington reportedly was burned. More than three hundred widows and orphans sought refuge in the town. A hastily constructed fort and earthworks, located at least partially on

Drawing by Baron Christoph von Graffenried of himself and John Lawson in Tuscarora captivity, 1711.

Lawson's property at the junction of Bath and Back Creeks, was meant to provide some measure of protection for residents and refugees. Meanwhile, efforts were undertaken in the Albemarle to aid the overwhelmed populace of Bath County. Thomas Pollock, the major general of the North Carolina militia, organized 150 men for a counterattack and marched to Bath. The force was supposed to join a group under the command of William Brice, who had raised approximately 50 to 60 men along the Neuse River. However, Pollock's men refused to venture out from Bath, forcing Brice to retreat to his fortified plantation. At that impasse, North Carolina pitifully sought assistance from Virginia, which despite promises, sent only small amounts of powder and cloth to North Carolina.

Desperate North Carolinians then turned to South Carolina, which quickly responded by raising money to finance a military expedition to go to the rescue of the northern province. John ("Tuscarora Jack") Barnwell led an expedition of 33 mounted whites and some 495 Indians, mostly Yamassee and Catawba, to North Carolina in January 1712. Late that month Barnwell reached the Neuse River above New Bern and began to attack fortified Tuscarora towns. After destroying several towns, killing Indians, and burning crops, Barnwell made his way to the Pamlico River at which point he decided to contact the North Carolinians before assaulting Catechna. After passing numerous "well ruined English plantations" and crossing several creeks that gave him "a world of trouble,"

Barnwell's force reached Bath on February 11 to the "incredible wonder and amazement of the poor distressed wretches" there, "who expressed such extremity of mad joy that it drew tears" from most of his men.[29]

Upon receiving supplies and reinforcements from North Carolinians, Barnwell in late February left the Pamlico garrisons to advance on Catechna. Finding that the Indians harbored several captives, Barnwell agreed to withdraw if the prisoners were released and the Tuscarora would discuss terms of a general truce. When the Tuscarora failed to comply fully, Barnwell besieged Catechna, but after ten days acceded to a treaty, in part to secure the freedom of the remaining prisoners and in part to avoid running out of supplies that had been promised but not delivered by the North Carolinians. As a result Barnwell incurred the censure of the North Carolina government for failing to destroy the Tuscarora. Despairing of a reward to compensate him for his services, Barnwell seized several Indians as slaves and returned with them to South Carolina. As a result of the breach of the treaty with the Tuscarora, the Indians renewed their attacks in the summer of 1712.

Again North Carolina sought the aid of South Carolina. At the same time Gov. Edward Hyde tried to organize an expedition from the Albemarle region to the Pamlico but fell victim to yellow fever in September 1712. However, Pollock as president of the council assumed leadership of the colony and proved an extremely competent executive. But the salvation of North Carolina was a second South Carolina military expedition. Despite the ill treatment accorded to Barnwell, the southern province sent James Moore in command of some thirty-three whites and almost a thousand Indians to North Carolina. The force reached the Neuse River in December 1712, and then marched to Bath. Finding no supplies, Moore continued on to the Albemarle area. Delayed by a severe winter marked by deep snows, the South Carolinians, reinforced by seventy to eighty North Carolina militia, finally attacked the Tuscarora in February 1713. Their objective was Fort Nohoroco (Neoheroka, Nookerooka), the principal Tuscarora stronghold at that time, which was located a few miles above Catechna on Contentnea Creek in present Greene County.

After three weeks of siege and fighting in March, Moore's force totally defeated the Tuscarora, killing, wounding, or capturing some 950, at the expense of 150 white and South Carolina Indian casualties. The power of the Tuscarora was crushed. Those who were not enslaved were relegated to a reservation in Bertie County or went north to New York to join their fellow Iroquois, the Five Nations. Before he left North Carolina, Moore had to deal with resistance offered by the Core and Machapunga, who attacked settlements along the Pamlico River and the area east of Bath. Even then roving bands of Indians kept the Pamlico region in turmoil until early 1715, when most agreed to surrender their land and move to a reservation near Lake Mattamuskeet. Still, as late as 1718, Gov. Charles Eden of North Carolina wrote from Bath, "a great Number [of] Indians neer Bath Town have already taken Some Captives and threaten the rest of the Inhabitants with Destruction." At the same time rangers policed the Neuse River and Core Sound area, even the environs of New Bern itself, to guard against Indian incursions.[30]

The defeat of the Tuscarora marked the beginning of an era of expansion in North Carolina, though it came at great cost. With the barrier posed by the Tuscarora broken, settlement of the southern coast and the interior proceeded rapidly. But the immediate effects of the Indian conflict were devastating—a high death toll; ravaged plantations; the disruption of public business occasioned by the loss of records; and the abandonment of New Bern and the scattering of Graffenried's settlement. Even the Albemarle, untouched by actual warfare, suffered privation. A large public debt and the issuance of paper currency by the government compounded the problems of the province. Nevertheless, the conclusion of the war brought an end to the political factionalism. Not until the 1740s did the southern counties again challenge the dominance of the Albemarle. Finally, the upheavals in the executive branch of the government during the first decade of the eighteenth century led the General Assembly to assert itself to a degree theretofore unknown, presaging the struggles between governors and legislatures that would characterize North Carolina politics for the remainder of the colonial era.[31]

The town of Bath struggled to rebound from the effects of the Tuscarora War. The Reverend John Urmstone, Anglican missionary, wrote sarcastically in 1714, "We expect to hear that famous city of Bath, consisting of 9 houses or rather cottages once stiled the Metropolis & Seat of Government will be totally deserted." Although exaggerated, his was a telling commentary on the impact of the conflict. Indeed, the J. B. Homann map of 1714, "Dominia Anglorum in America," showed greater settlement activity west of Bath than in the town itself. Happily for the future of Bath, Charles Eden, who succeeded Hyde as governor of North Carolina in 1714, decided to make his home in the town, the General Assembly in 1715 enacted legislation to revive the town, and English authorities designated Bath as an official port of entry for shipping in the southern part of North Carolina.[32]

NOTES

1. David Beers Quinn, *North America from Earliest Discovery to First Settlements: The Norse Voyages to 1612* (New York: Harper and Row, 1977), 144-147, 237-238, 282-283; Woodbury Lowery, *The Spanish Settlements within the Present Limits of the United States, 1513-1574*, 2 vols. (New York: Russell and Russell, Inc., 1959), 1:153-168, 373-375; Clifford S. Lewis, S. J. Loomie, and Albert J. Loomie, *The Spanish Jesuit Mission in Virginia, 1570-1572* (Chapel Hill: University of North Carolina Press, 1953); L. A. Vigneras, "A Spanish Discovery of North Carolina in 1566," *North Carolina Historical Review* 46 (autumn 1969): 398-414; Alan D. Watson, "The European Discovery of North Carolina," (paper presented at the Schiele Museum, Gastonia, N.C., 1984).

2. David Leroy Corbitt, ed., *Explorations, Descriptions, and Attempted Settlements of Carolina, 1584-1590*, rev. ed. (Raleigh: State Department of Archives and History, 1953), 139-145; Samuel Eliot Morison, *The European Discovery of America. The Northern Voyages, A.D. 500-1600* (New York: Oxford University Press, 1971), 282-316.

3. Quinn, *North America from Earliest Discovery*, 362-364; David Beers Quinn, *Set Fair for Roanoke: Voyages and Colonies, 1584-1606* (Chapel Hill: University of North Carolina Press, 1985); David N. Durant, *Ralegh's Lost Colony* (New York: Atheneum, 1981).

4. Wilson Angley, "The Bonner House Vicinity of Bath, North Carolina: Four Hundred Years of Its History" (report, Research Branch, Division of Archives and History, Raleigh, February 1979), 1-2. The Gerhard Mercator Hondius map of 1606, *Virginiae Item et Floridae*, calls the village "Cotan," while Willem Blaeu labeled it "Secotan" on his *Virginiae parties australis et Floridae* in 1640.

5. Angley, "Bonner House Vicinity of Bath," 2.

6. Hugh T. Lefler, "Promotional Literature of the Southern Colonies," *Journal of Southern History* 33 (February 1967): 15; Lindley S. Butler, "The Early Settlement of Carolina," *Virginia Magazine of History and Biography* 79 (January 1971): 20-28; Paul E. Kopperman, "Profile of Failure: The Carolana Project, 1629-1640," *North Carolina Historical Review* 59 (winter 1982): 1-23.

7. Daniel W. Fagg Jr., "Sleeping Not with the King's Grant: A Rereading of Some Proprietary Documents, 1663-1667," *North Carolina Historical Review* 48 (spring 1971): 171-185; Lawrence Lee, *The Lower Cape Fear in Colonial Days* (Chapel Hill: University of North Carolina Press, 1965), 41-53.

8. William L. Saunders, ed., *The Colonial Records of North Carolina*, 10 vols. (Raleigh: State of North Carolina, 1886-1890), 1:391; "Seth Sothel," in William S. Powell, ed., *Dictionary of North Carolina Biography*, 6 vols. (Chapel Hill: University of North Carolina Press, 1979-1996), 5:399-401; Lindley S. Butler, "The Governors of Albemarle County, 1663-1689," *North Carolina Historical Review* 46 (summer 1969): 295-299; Hugh T. Lefler and William S. Powell, *Colonial North Carolina: A History* (New York: Charles Scribner's Sons, 1973), 56.

9. Angley, "Bonner House Vicinity of Bath," 8-10.

10. David Leroy Corbitt, ed., *The Formation of the North Carolina Counties, 1663-1943* (Raleigh: State Department of Archives and History, 1950), 18-19.

11. Book 2, pp. 312-313 (microfilm), Beaufort County Deeds, State Archives, Office of Archives and History, Raleigh; Herbert R. Paschal Jr., *A History of Colonial Bath* (Raleigh: Edwards and Broughton, 1955), 4-5; Martha W. McCartney, "History [of] Bath Town, North Carolina," (Williamsburg: Virginia Research Center for Archaeology, 1978), unpaginated.

12. Mattie Erma Edwards Parker, ed., *North Carolina Charters and Constitutions, 1578-1698*, vol. 1 of *The Colonial Records of North Carolina* [*Second Series*] (Raleigh: Carolina Charter Tercentenary Commission, 1963), 85-86, 116, 148; Walter Clark, ed., *The State Records of North Carolina*, 16 vols. (11-26) (Raleigh: State of North Carolina, 1895-1906), 25:120.

13. Saunders, *Colonial Records*, 1:100-101, 229; 4:424.

14. Book 1, p. 49 (microfilm), Beaufort County Deeds; Paschal, *History of Colonial Bath*, 5, 7; Angley, "Bonner House Vicinity of Bath," 12-13. England used the Julian calendar until 1752, when it switched to the Gregorian calendar. In the former system, the new year began on March 25. Thus February 11, 1705, Old Style or Julian became February 11, 1706, New Style or Gregorian.

15. John Lawson, *A New Voyage to Carolina*, ed. by Hugh T. Lefler (Chapel Hill: University of North Carolina Press, 1967), xi-xv, 67; Angley, "Bonner House Vicinity of Bath," 10.

16. Lawson, *New Voyage to Carolina*, xviii-xxii; Saunders, *Colonial Records*, 2:756; Paschal, *History of Colonial Bath*, 8; Angley, "Bonner House Vicinity of Bath," 15.

17. Lawson, *New Voyage to Carolina*, lii-liv; "John Lawson," in Powell, *Dictionary of North Carolina Biography*, 4:35; Paschal, *History of Colonial Bath*, 8.

18. Hoxie Neale Fairchild, *The Noble Savage: A Study in Romantic Naturalism* (New York: Columbia University Press, 1928), 2; A. L. Diket, "The Noble Savage Convention as Epitomized in John Lawson's *A New Voyage to Carolina*," *North Carolina Historical Review* 43 (autumn 1966): 413-429.

19. Clark, *State Records*, 23:73; Angley, "Bonner House Vicinity of Bath," 13; Paschal, *History of Colonial Bath*, 5, 7; Gerald W. Butler, site manager, Historic Bath State Historic Site, letter to author, February 6, 2001; Richard Lawrence, Underwater Archaeology Unit, Office of State Archaeology, Division of Archives and History, telephone conversation with author, November 16, 2001.

20. Saunders, *Colonial Records*, 1:715, 772; Paschal, *History of Colonial Bath*, 8-9; McCartney, "History [of] Bath Town."

21. Lawson, *New Voyage to Carolina*, 274-275; Angley, "Bonner House Vicinity of Bath," 10, 13-15.

22. Book 1, pp. 64, 78, 162 (microfilm), Beaufort County Deeds; Angley, "Bonner House Vicinity of Bath," 15.

23. William S. Price, ed., *North Carolina Higher-Court Records, 1709-1723*, vol. 5 of *The Colonial Records of North Carolina* [*Second Series*] (Raleigh: Division of Archives and History, Department of Cultural Resources, 1974), 23, 51, 481; Book 1, p. 53 (microfilm), Beaufort County Deeds; Paschal, *History of Colonial Bath*, 10.

24. Mattie Erma Edwards Parker, ed., *North Carolina Higher-Court Records, 1670-1696*, vol. 2 of *The Colonial Records of North Carolina* [*Second Series*] (Raleigh: State Department of Archives and History, 1968), xxx-lxii; Lefler and Powell, *Colonial North Carolina*, 44-55; Butler, "Governors of Albemarle County," 281-299.

25. For Cary and Cary's Rebellion, see William S. Price, ed., *North Carolina Higher-Court Records, 1702-1708*, vol. 4 of *The Colonial Records of North Carolina* [*Second Series*] (Raleigh: Division of Archives and History, Department of Cultural Resources, 1974), xxiv-xxx; Price, *North Carolina Higher-Court Records, 1709-1723*, xxi-xxv; Saunders, *Colonial Records*, 1:803-804; "Thomas Cary," in Powell, *Dictionary of North Carolina Biography*, 1:338-339; Louis P. Towles, "Cary's

Rebellion and the Emergence of Thomas Pollock," *Journal of the Association of Historians in North Carolina* 4 (fall 1996): 36-58; C. Wingate Reed, *Beaufort County: Two Centuries of Its History* (n.p., 1962), 57-64; Charles Bryan Lowery, "Class, Politics, Rebellion and Regional Development in Proprietary North Carolina (1697-1720)" (Ph.D. diss., University of Florida, 1979), 150-202.

26. Reed, *Beaufort County*, 63.

27. Paschal, *History of Colonial Bath*, 19. Of course, the ensuing Tuscarora War that began in September 1711 added to the confusion caused by Cary's Rebellion and contributed to the destruction of public records.

28. For the Tuscarora War, *see* Price, *North Carolina Higher-Court Records, 1707-1723*, xxv-xxx; Lefler and Powell, *Colonial North Carolina*, 64-80; Reed, *Beaufort County*, 65-75; Thomas C. Parramore, "The Tuscarora Ascendancy," *North Carolina Historical Review* 59 (autumn 1982): 307-326; Herbert R. Paschal Jr., "Tuscarora Indians in North Carolina" (master's thesis, University of North Carolina, 1953).

29. "The Tuscarora Expedition: Letters of Colonel John Barnwell," *South Carolina Magazine of History and Biography* 9 (January 1908): 40-41.

30. Joseph W. Barnwell, ed., "The Second Tuscarora Expedition," *South Carolina Magazine of History and Biography* 10 (January 1909): 40; Saunders, *Colonial Records*, 2:308-309; Price, *North Carolina Higher-Court Records, 1709-1723*, 188; Alan D. Watson, *A History of New Bern and Craven County* (New Bern: Tryon Palace Commission, 1987), 21.

31. Saunders, *Colonial Records*, 1:860, 881-882; Price, *North Carolina Higher-Court Records, 1709-1723*, xxxi; Christine Styrna, "The Tuscarora War, 1711-1713: The Struggle for Power, Profit, and Survival" (paper presented to the American Society of Ethnohistory, Williamsburg, Va., 1988).

32. Saunders, *Colonial Records*, 2:vi, 144, 229; Clark, *State Records*, 23:73-79; "Charles Eden," in Powell, *Dictionary of North Carolina Biography*, 2:134; McCartney, "History [of] Bath Town."

2

Governance and Politics

Bath represented the belated beginning of urbanization in North Carolina and only briefly enjoyed its distinction as the sole town in North Carolina. Under the guidance of Graffenried and Lawson, New Bern appeared at the confluence of the Neuse and Trent Rivers in 1710. Devastated by the Tuscarora War, New Bern finally revived by 1730. Before the end of the Tuscarora War, Edenton and Beaufort had been founded, though they were not chartered by the legislature until 1722 and 1723, respectively. Brunswick Town arose in the 1720s in the midst of the permanent settlement of the Lower Cape Fear, joined by Wilmington a decade later. A host of even smaller towns or villages, including Hertford, Nixonton, Windsor, and Kinston, supplemented the major urban centers. As settlement spread to the interior, other towns appeared, including Halifax, Tarboro, Cross Creek, Campbellton, Hillsborough, Salisbury, Charlotte, and Salem.

Although Edenton, New Bern, and Wilmington—the three most populous towns at the time of the Revolution—each contained no more than a thousand people, and urban residents throughout the colony probably constituted no more than 2 percent of North Carolina's population, towns played an indispensable role in the governmental, political, economic, and social development of North Carolina. Most served as county seats, the focus of local government and politics. All appeared, usually deliberately but sometimes accidentally, as centers of trade. Coastal towns were the avenues to the outside world. Central and western towns helped to funnel goods to markets along the coast or in Virginia and South Carolina. Beyond their importance as commercial conduits, towns clustered people together, if only in small numbers in North Carolina, which served to promote the impact of religion and foster educational and cultural opportunities, as well as to heighten political awareness. As the Lords Proprietors had early recognized, towns were essential to the development of the colony.

Early Settlement of Bath

The town commissioners constituted the most immediate and recognizable authority in Bath. When the General Assembly in 1715 revised and codified the laws of North Carolina, it confirmed the incorporation of Bath and appointed new commissioners or trustees—John Porter, Joel Martin, Thomas Harding, and John Drinkwater—to govern the town. The law required a resurvey of Bath, reserving land for a church, market, and courthouse, and directed that unmarked land be laid off in half-acre lots and streets by the commissioners. Apparently the initial surveyors had erred by creating lots of a half-acre and four poles (approximately one-fourth of an acre). The price of a lot was thirty shillings. Although all lots in the resurvey were limited to one-half of an acre, owners of property along Bath (Old Town) Creek were allowed to purchase the land between Main (Water, Bay) Street and the creek that fronted their lots for an additional ten shillings.[1]

A plat of Bath in 1717 revealed the results of the resurvey. The commissioners divided the town into seventy-one lots. According to law, they set aside lots 61 and 62 for a church and courthouse, respectively. Main (Water) Street ran north to south beside Bath Creek from Back (Adams) Creek to the town limits, and in turn was paralleled to the east by Church Street and then King (the "long") Street. Church Street extended from the northern limits of Bath about two-thirds the length of the town where it terminated in a cross street. King Street constituted the easternmost bounds of the town (as well as a race track on occasion) and the road to Edenton. Running east to west were Front Street, which bordered Back Creek and connected Main and King Streets, and Craven and Carteret (sometimes called Cartwright) Streets, which also linked Main and King but intersected Church Street. By law the principal streets were supposed to be one hundred feet wide. Only Main Street satisfied that stipulation; King and Craven were sixty-six feet wide; Carteret, fifty-two feet wide.[2]

Trying to promote the settlement of Bath as opposed to speculation in town property, the General Assembly required each lot owner to build "a good substantial habitable house," with minimum dimensions of fifteen by fifteen feet, or, at least, to undertake the construction of such a house within twelve months of the purchase of the lot. Otherwise the sale would be deemed void, and the lot would be made available for repurchase, a decision left to the precinct or county court. In practice, however, that legal stricture apparently was loosely enforced, for rarely were lots forfeited, and those mainly before 1740. Christopher Gale lost lot 13 for "not complying as the . . . [law] directs," and it was resold in 1716 to

Joseph Morgan. When Michael McDonagh, town commissioner and shipwright, allowed lots 49, 50, and 51 to lapse, the Reverend John Garzia purchased the properties in 1735. Although failing immediately to improve their lots and thereby relinquishing their claims, Mary Aldershire and Alexander Hamilton repurchased their original lots.[3]

The legislature also acted to promote a pleasing aesthetic appearance for Bath as well as to ensure the safety and healthfulness of the town. The statute of 1715 required lot owners within a month of the passage of the legislation to clear their property of trees, underbrush, and shrubs that might be "Offensive" to the residents of Bath. William Sigley was appointed by the law to clear lots of those who neglected their responsibility. If Sigley refused or was unavailable, the commissioners of the town were authorized to appoint someone to act in his stead. There is no evidence that the services of Sigley, later a commissioner, or anyone, were needed to fell trees and eliminate undergrowth.[4]

The General Assembly evidenced concern for the proper use of land and the preservation of the waterfront vista of Bath. In order to protect the beauty of the town, owners of waterfront lots along Bath Creek were prohibited from erecting storehouses or buildings along the creek except for cellars or vaults whose height was limited to ten feet. Later, in 1723, the ban was repealed because it was "found very prejudiciall to trade and to the Inhabitants of the . . . Town in General." In addition, those owning waterfront lots were permitted to build wharves into the water "to the Edge of the Channel" of the creek. Legislation in 1745 clarified the earlier statute, empowering owners of waterfront lots to construct stores, warehouses, and other buildings "for carrying on their Trade and Commerce." Business had trumped beauty. The General Assembly learned from the experience, later requiring owners of waterfront lots in New Bern and Edenton to build wharves or warehouses on their property within two years or the land would be made available to the public for improvement.[5]

Government and Infrastructure in Early Bath

The enforcement of these laws and the governance of Bath were generally entrusted to town commissioners. Early Americans adopted various approaches to urban governance. New Englanders used the town meeting, superficially at least a democratic means of regulating urban affairs. Mid-Atlantic towns, including New York, Philadelphia, and New Brunswick, New Jersey, along with southern communities such as Norfolk, Virginia, used the municipal corporation, patterned after the English model chartered by the Crown.[6] Municipal government in North Carolina, however, including that of Bath, traditionally consisted of commissioners, trustees, or directors appointed by the General Assembly when

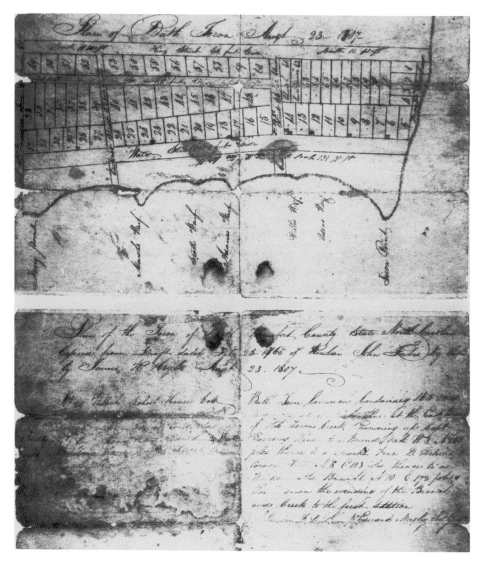

Plan of Bath town lots, 1807, from a draft dated 1766.

chartering the towns. The number of commissioners ranged from three in the case of Bath originally, and four for Edenton, to as many as eleven for Campbellton and Salisbury, but fluctuated over time as towns' laws were amended. The commissioners usually constituted a closed, self-perpetuating board. Upon the death or resignation of a member, the remaining commissioners were empowered to name a replacement.[7]

In the incorporation of Bath in 1715, the General Assembly resorted to a slight aberration from the norm of self-perpetuation. That legislation required remaining commissioners and the justices of the peace of the precinct or county court in whose jurisdiction the town lay—Beaufort in the case of Bath—jointly to name successors to deceased or resigned commissioners. The General Assembly also applied the joint-replacement principle to Beaufort in 1723 and 1770, to Woodstock (in Hyde County) in 1738, and to Salisbury in 1770. However, when addressing Bath in 1745, the General Assembly resorted to the standard approach for replacing commissioners. It appointed five new commissioners for the town—Michael Coutanch (Coutanche), Benjamin Peyton, John Rieusset, Robert Boyd, and Daniel Blinn—who were made solely self-perpetuating, independent of the Beaufort County Court.[8]

The General Assembly eventually offered a measure of self-government to certain towns. In 1740 it allowed residents of Wilmington to nominate five men to serve as commissioners from whom the governor would select three. Five years later the legislature authorized the freemen of Wilmington to elect their town commissioners. In 1748 the same privilege was extended to New Bern. Residents of Brunswick and Martinsborough (present Greenville) were granted the right to elect their commissioners in 1767 and 1774, respectively. Limited information about Bath indicates that, like most North Carolina towns, it retained the self-perpetuating board of commissioners until the Revolution.[9]

The regulatory authority of the town commissioners in the larger municipalities in colonial North Carolina embraced most aspects of urban life, including oversight of public structures, management of the market, trash disposal, fire prevention, and the confinement of livestock. In Bath, the scope of commissioner activity appeared more limited. Although a county courthouse and jail were erected in town, responsibility for those buildings fell to the Beaufort County Court. However, legislation in 1715 called for allotting acreage in Bath for a "Town-House & a Market Place," whose oversight would have been entrusted to the commissioners. As was the case initially with New Bern and Wilmington, whose courthouses were raised on pillars, Bath may have used an area beneath the courthouse for the sale of meat and produce rather than construct a separate market house.[10] Most likely, a market house was never built, for the small number of residents in Bath could have furnished themselves with food by means of gardens and livestock adjacent to their houses, and would not have needed a public market.

The 1715 statute also empowered the commissioners "to Remove all Nuisances" within the limits of the town. Nuisances broadly represented that which was obnoxious to the community, whether it was offensive by smell or appearance, obstructive, or dangerous. In the larger towns commissioners ordered the removal of naval stores and lumber that hindered traffic in the streets; oversaw the collection of trash, which occasioned the appointment of a town scavenger in Wilmington; and determined the location of necessary houses, or privies. Again, in

Bath the pace of life and course of business were more leisurely and probably required little intervention from the commissioners.[11]

The Bath town commissioners by law also assumed responsibility for the "inspection and . . . care of the town common." The commons, located on the northern bounds of the town, had early been laid off and surveyed. The General Assembly in 1729 extended legal recognition to the area as the town commons and directed that the land remain "perpetually for the Use and Benefit of the Inhabitants of Bath-Town, under such Restrictions and Regulations as is or shall be appointed for Town Commons." Regulations for the town commons were never detailed, however. Sixteen years later the legislature required the Bath commissioners to resurvey the commons at the expense of the residents and mark the bounds, so that those living in Bath would not trespass on its adjoining lands.[12]

Arguably the most pervasive difficulty facing residents of colonial towns was the presence of free-roaming livestock, particularly hogs. The General Assembly warned those who lived in Bath to keep their hogs in "close Penns or houses." The stipulation in the 1715 law that forbade Bath inhabitants to allow hogs to run at large was repeated many times in subsequent legislation that incorporated towns in North Carolina. The legislature reiterated the provisions of the Bath law relative to hogs in a general statutory directive in 1723 that required all urban residents in North Carolina to pen their hogs securely. In addition to hogs, cattle and goats probably wandered the town, playing havoc with yards and gardens; dogs, the most ubiquitous of the animals, were also bothersome. The General Assembly in 1756 forbade homeowners in New Bern to keep more than one cow, one calf, one horse, and six sheep "running at large" in the town; legislation for Wilmington permitted town commissioners to enact ordinances to control livestock and to fine violators. Despite many complaints in Wilmington about loose animals, the few levies imposed by the commissioners indicated that efforts to restrain animals were largely in vain. No doubt that was true of Bath in the case of hogs.[13]

Fencing was viewed as a means to possibly prevent wandering livestock from invading towns. The legislature in 1731 authorized the Edenton town commissioners to erect a fence around the town and its commons, and passed similar legislation for Bath in 1745 and New Bern in 1748. The statute for Bath instructed the town commissioners to levy an annual tax for the construction and maintenance of a fence with gates to surround the town. The law required two gates, one sufficiently large to admit carts and a smaller gate to allow riders on horseback to enter and exit the town. The fences deteriorated quickly, necessitating legislation in 1756 to repair the posts and rails in Edenton and New Bern. Still, by 1769, according to maps prepared by Claude J. Sauthier, the fences around Edenton and New Bern had largely disappeared. However, the fence around Bath appears largely intact.[14]

In addition to controlling livestock and maintaining fences, clearing and repairing streets in towns, as well as the roads throughout the countryside, proved an ongoing difficulty for colonials. Ordinarily all male taxables (white males sixteen years of age and older, and black males twelve years of age and older) in colonial North Carolina were responsible for constructing and maintaining roads and bridges in their respective counties. County courts divided the taxables into road companies, and for each company appointed a road overseer, who called the men to work and supervised their activity. Legislation in 1740, repeated in 1745, exempted the inhabitants of Bath from working on the public roads in Beaufort County, provided that they kept the streets of the town in repair and lots cleared of trash. The General Assembly commonly relieved the men living in towns of responsibility for county roads if they took care of the municipal streets. In larger towns the commissioners appointed overseers for the streets; in small ones, like Bath, the county court appointed the overseers. John Brown, a former town constable, was appointed overseer in 1761 for Bath by the Beaufort County Court.[15]

Construction of a Courthouse at Bath

As the only town in Beaufort Precinct (County after 1739), and conveniently situated on water, Bath constituted the obvious site for public gatherings in the county, including meetings of the court of pleas and quarter sessions, militia musters, and elections for members of the General Assembly and vestries. A court, apparently for Bath County, but eventually for Beaufort Precinct, met in Bath as early as October 1706, and continued to convene in the town in subsequent years, though in private homes.

In 1715, the General Assembly ordered the construction of a courthouse in Bath to serve both Beaufort and Hyde Precincts, whose governments were combined and served by one set of officials until 1729. The legislation empowered the magistrates to levy a tax to pay for the structure, in what was apparently the first extant statute in North Carolina authorizing a precinct court to impose a tax, though not until the precincts had recovered from the effects of the Tuscarora War. In 1722, the legislature, cognizant that the magistrates in most precincts in North Carolina held court in private residences, designated permanent sites for precinct court meetings. At that time the legislature reiterated its directive that the Beaufort and Hyde Precinct Courts should meet in Bath.[16]

The date of the construction of a courthouse in Bath is unknown. It may have been erected as early as 1720 in consequence of the 1715 statute, but more likely construction began in the aftermath of the legislation in 1722, when the General Assembly ordered the justices of each precinct to purchase an acre of land on which to construct a courthouse, and authorized them to impose a tax for that purpose.

Although the justices of Beaufort and Hyde Precincts collected a tax for the construction of a courthouse in Bath, the levy was insufficient to pay for that structure and an accompanying jail, which the General Assembly decided was "absolutely necessary by Reason of the heavy Complaints from the provost Marshal and divers[e] of the Inhabitants of . . . [Bath] County." Therefore the legislature in 1723 authorized the imposition of an additional tax on the residents of Beaufort and Hyde Precincts to build the jail, as well as an annual levy to maintain and repair the courthouse and jail. If constructed by 1723, as this statute seems to suggest, the courthouse in Bath may well have been the second in the colony, following one built in Edenton. However, at the same time, other precincts were in the process of building courthouses.[17]

The jail at Bath was destroyed by an act of arson in February 1733/34. Sixteen-year-old George Lewis and Eleanor Carty were charged with setting the fire, in which Richard Moore, a prisoner, perished. The accused were transported to Edenton to stand trial in the General Court. Testimony revealed that Carty's intent in torching the jail was to kill Moore, for reasons unspecified.[18]

Bath briefly lost its distinction as the seat of Beaufort County when the General Assembly in 1755 acknowledged the petition of several county residents who complained that the town was not centrally located, making it difficult for them to attend court, elections, and musters. The legislature moved the location of the courthouse to land on the north side of Pamlico River belonging to Thomas Bonner Jr., site of the future town of Washington, and named commissioners, including Edward Salter, to contract for the erection of a new courthouse and jail. The justices of the Beaufort court were authorized to impose a tax on county inhabitants to pay for the buildings, and were ordered to move to the new location upon their completion. The commissioners engaged Frederick Hargott to build a courthouse, prison, pillory, and stocks.[19]

However, a majority of the county justices, led by Robert Palmer and Michael Coutanche, who lived in or near Bath, objected to the relocation of the county seat. By a seven to four vote, they defeated a proposal at the June 1756 term of court to assess a levy to raise £190 to pay for the courthouse complex, claiming that the justices lacked the authority. When Edward Salter noted at the September term of court that the buildings had been finished, and moved to reconvene in the new courthouse, the opposing justices by a vote of six to five still refused, declaring that they ought not adjourn to a "place and Courthouse which in no ways can be deemed the publicks until a tax is laid to pay the same and many more material reasons might be given." The minority then turned for redress to the General Assembly that met in September and October 1756. The legislature, observing that the Beaufort court had "contemptuously" refused to impose a tax and move to the new location, ordered the sheriff to collect the levy and directed the next court to convene in the courthouse on Bonner's land. The Beaufort magistrates obediently met in the new courthouse for the December 1756 term of court.[20]

Bath again became the seat of Beaufort County when the General Assembly in 1760 erected Pitt County from Beaufort, and required that meetings of the Beaufort County Court be moved from Bonner's land back to Bath. All suits, returns of processes, and witness appearances were to proceed without interruption in Bath. In preparation for the change, the justices ordered Michael Coutanche to employ workmen to repair the jail in Bath. Although by law the relocation to Bath was supposed to occur in January 1761, the magistrates delayed the move until June of that year. By 1766 the old courthouse and jail had so deteriorated that, according to the General Assembly, "the Courts cannot be held therein, nor Prisoners detained." Therefore the legislature appointed Palmer, John Barrow, Thomas Respess, Wyriot Ormond, and Thomas Bonner commissioners to contract for the construction of a new courthouse, jail, pillory, and stocks. Bath remained the county seat through 1785, when it was superseded by Washington, informally founded by James Bonner in 1775-1776 and incorporated in 1782.[21]

Although the exact location of the original courthouse in Bath remains uncertain, presumably it was built on Lot 62, designated on the plat of the town for such a structure. However, surveying errors may have occasioned the encroachment of the courthouse (and presumably jail) on Lot 61, the designated location for a church, which might account for the fact that the church, St. Thomas, was built in the center of Craven Street. According to the Sauthier map of 1769, the second courthouse was sited on the waterfront at the end of Craven Street between Main Street and Bath Creek. The jail stood a short distance northwest, closer to the water.[22]

In the absence of a physical description of the government buildings in Bath, the directive of the General Assembly and similar structures in other counties might serve as guides. By statute in 1722 the legislature mandated that the courthouse be twenty-four feet long and sixteen feet wide. More specifically, the following plan for the Currituck County courthouse in 1723 might have exemplified the plan for the early Bath courthouse:

> thirty feet in length eighteen feet in width with a
> fashionable over Jet framed Worke Standing on Cedar Blocks
> the roof to be Shingled with Cypress Shingles the Sides and
> ends with boards the floors to be raised two feet from the
> ground with plank two Barrs on the Said Floor from Side to
> Side two feet and an half asunder and all that part of the
> house to be ceiled workmanlike Judges Chair Benches and
> Clerks Table the upper floor plained Joynted and Close layed
> the frame of the house to be plained and made Smooth with
> Stairs from floor to floor with Sash windowes not less than
> eight feet pitch.[23]

Governance of Early Bath

The Beaufort Precinct Court of Pleas and Quarter Sessions convened at the courthouse in Bath. The precinct or county court represented not only a judicial but also an administrative agency. It was composed of justices of the peace, or magistrates, appointed by the governor, any three of whom constituted a quorum at its quarterly sessions. The court assumed cognizance over many criminal and civil matters; appeals might be taken to the General Court of the colony. Administrative concerns and matters of probate absorbed much of the court's time, however, for the justices certified and recorded deeds, bills of sale, and wills, recorded marks or brands, and probated estates, which entailed an inventory of the assets, an accounting of the debits, and the appointment of administrators or executors of the property. The court also supervised orphans, apprenticing poorer children and finding guardians for the wealthier, and protected indentured servants. The jurisdiction of the court included maintenance of public buildings—the courthouse, jail, and warehouses—and the power of taxation. The magistrates oversaw local transportation, directing the construction and maintenance of roads and bridges, appointing road overseers for those purposes, and establishing ferries. The court also regulated taverns, licensing the businesses and determining the rates of fare. The county sheriff, nominated by the justices but appointed by the governor, and constables, appointed by the magistrates, executed the judicial and administrative directives of the court. In fact, the county court exercised almost complete control over the lives of those who lived within its jurisdiction, and most people rarely felt the impress of any other governmental agency unless they lived in an incorporated town.[24]

For law enforcement and administrative purposes Bath obtained the services of a constable. The county courts annually appointed constables, who served one-year terms and were exempted from reappointment for five years thereafter unless they voluntarily agreed to accept the office. The number of constables no doubt bore some relation to the density of population and geographic extent of the counties. From five to nine sufficed for Hyde, Carteret, and Onslow just before the Revolution, but Tryon needed eighteen in 1769 and Rowan thirty-six in 1774. Towns and villages always benefited from constabulary protection. The larger urban areas, Wilmington, New Bern, and Edenton, merited two or more constables. Smaller Beaufort and Brunswick each needed one. Similarly, the Beaufort County Court appointed a single constable for Bath. John Brown served the town in 1757; Adam Jones, in 1758; and Peter Caila, from 1759 to 1761.[25]

Constables acted both as law enforcement officers and administrative officials of the county court. In the former capacity, constables were responsible essentially for keeping the peace—preventing fights, breaking up altercations, and sometimes punishing those who violated the law. With sheriffs, they also sought suspected

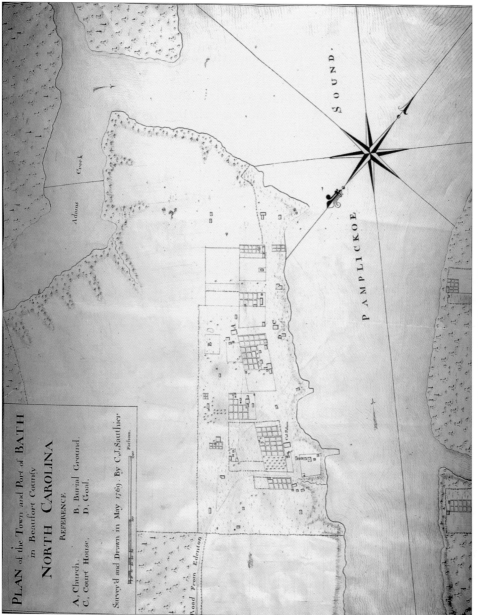

Plan of Bath, 1769, by C. J. Sauthier.

37

criminals, sometimes going beyond their districts in search of lawbreakers. The justices of the peace demanded the presence of constables at meetings of the county courts in order to maintain decorum among the occasionally unruly crowds. Constables delivered warrants, assisted the grand and petit juries, and in general served the needs of the magistrates. In their administrative capacity, constables formed a critical cog in the tax collection process in the colony by helping justices of the peace to compile lists of persons upon whom taxes were levied. Moreover, constables summoned single parents to bring orphans or illegitimate children to court for apprenticeship, sold estates at public auction, and called upon road overseers to settle accounts of fines collected from negligent workers.[26]

Constabulary duties in urban areas mainly entailed notifying heads of families to send their male taxables to work on the streets of the towns and levying warrants of distress on the property of those who failed to obey the summons. Additional demands upon constables in towns included collecting taxes, policing the commercial activities of slaves, and maintaining an orderly atmosphere on Sundays for those who attended church. Given the size of Bath, the demands imposed on its constables were probably light. Still, the job was potentially dangerous, particularly when the constable had to break up tavern brawls. Constables also encountered a traditional colonial aversion to interference in private affairs. That attitude, combined with the constables' often lowly socioeconomic status, which compromised their ability to command respect, may well have led to a policy of circumspection in dealing with the populace.[27]

The General Assembly, the Beaufort County Court, and the town commissioners shared the governance of Bath. The legislature broadly determined the parameters of municipal government, requiring the survey and sale of lots, appointing commissioners or altering the mode of the selection of commissioners, and addressing such issues as a town commons and fencing. The Beaufort County Court initially assumed partial responsibility for replacing town commissioners, controlled the courthouse and jail in Bath, and appointed street overseers and constables for the town who were answerable to the county magistrates. The town commissioners directed the survey of town property, sold lots, took charge of the commons, erected and maintained the town fence, and possessed the authority to ensure the safety and welfare of the inhabitants of Bath.

Bath not only constituted the site for meetings of the county court but also assumed a provincial significance when the governor's executive council and the General Assembly met in the town. Before the establishment of a permanent capital in North Carolina, governors or executives of the colony convened the legislature at locations of their discretion. Meetings initially were held in private homes, but after the appearance of towns, urban sites were the most logical gathering places. Though small, they offered more extensive lodging facilities than did private homes.

Although Bath was the first town in North Carolina, soon after its founding Edenton was deemed the "metropolis" of the province and served as the de facto capital. But as settlement spread southward along the coast, eventually to the Cape Fear in the 1720s, the great distance that had to be traversed to Edenton, punctuated by several rivers that necessitated ferry crossings, proved formidable for those in the southern portion of the colony. Thus governors convened the council and legislature in Bath, New Bern, and Wilmington, sometimes for political purposes, but mainly to render the burden of travel more equitable, until New Bern was designated the permanent capital in 1766.

The governor—who represented the proprietors and, after 1729, the Crown upon the purchase of the Carolinas by King George II from the proprietors—and the General Assembly constituted the basic framework of colonial government. A bicameral body, the General Assembly consisted of an upper house and a lower house, or the House of Commons. The upper house or council consisted of twelve men nominated by the governor but appointed by the Crown and Privy Council in England. They served as an advisory board for the governor, sat as the upper house of the colonial legislature, and with the governor constituted the chancery court, the highest court of appeal in the colony. Theoretically councilors were men of esteem, education, and wealth, though over the years, especially toward the Revolution, a number of placemen sat on the board. Robert Palmer, a resident of Bath and member of the council from 1764 to 1775, represented both groups, for he was not only wealthy but also surveyor general of the colony and collector of customs for the Port of Bath. Whatever their circumstances, the councilors usually supported the governor and opposed the lower house in the ongoing confrontations between the executive and the General Assembly.[28]

On four occasions—October 3, 1735, February 29-March 9, 1743/4, March 12-15, 1745/6, and April 3-14, 1752—Gov. Gabriel Johnston (1734-1752) convened his council in Bath. In those meetings, the governor and council spent most of their time grappling with matters involving land, principally approving warrants and patents, and settling disputes over land titles. Much time was absorbed in hearings that involved the claims of speculator Henry McCulloh about the survey of his lands in western North Carolina. The council also heard reports from the receiver general of the quitrents of the colony, including not only the amount of moneys obtained but also the difficulties involved in collecting the land tax. Additionally, the governor with the advice and consent of the council appointed justices of the peace for various counties, issued writs of election for towns and counties, and entertained a complaint from a Chowan Indian that reservation lands belonging to the Chowan had been illegally sold.[29]

The General Assembly in Bath

Governor Johnston first brought the General Assembly to Bath on February 21, 1743/44, for what proved to be a short, contentious, and unproductive session. In his opening address to a joint meeting of the legislature, the governor asked the lawmakers to consider two controversial matters—sinking or retiring the outstanding paper currency in the colony, and fixing a permanent site for the government of North Carolina. The two houses immediately busied themselves with drafting addresses to the governor. The lower house as customary engaged in committee work, admitted tardy members, approved petitions for exemptions of infirm persons from tax payments and road work, and prepared bills for consideration. The upper and lower houses, always at loggerheads, disagreed over the terms of a bill for sinking currency, while neither was willing to initiate legislation to consider the controversial matter of a capital.[30]

Meanwhile, the upper house took umbrage at the lower house's decision to alter its mode of address when sending messages to the upper house. Rather than "May it please your Honours," the lower house substituted "Gentlemen of His Majesty's Council," a strong intimation that the lower house did not consider the upper house a part of the legislature, but an arm of the executive. In effect, the lower house claimed sole legislative privileges for itself, an argument that lower houses throughout the colonies, particularly in South Carolina, advanced repeatedly but without real effect in the quarter century preceding the Revolution. The upper house deemed the change an "affront and indignity . . . put on foot by some evil disposed persons to destroy the harmony and good understanding that has hitherto subsisted between the two Houses thereby to serve some sinister ends." Thus the upper house refused to transact business with the lower house until the usual style of address was adopted. When the lower house remained intransigent, Governor Johnston dissolved the General Assembly on March 8, 1744.[31]

Johnston again convened the General Assembly in Bath from April 2 to April 15, 1752. In his opening address to the legislature, the governor sought legislation "promoting religion, and Virtue and Suppressing vices and immorality, which are come to such a dreadful height in This Province." He particularly called attention to "the barbarous and inhuman manner of boxing which so much prevails among the lower sort of people," and called upon the legislature "to put a Stop to such bloody horrid quarrels." Although the General Assembly failed to address matters of religion and morality, it did enact nine bills to which the governor assented, including measures to license traders, to facilitate navigation, to create Orange County, and to erect a toll bridge in New Hanover County. Tension remained between the upper and lower houses, however, for the latter refused to approve a questionable travel reimbursement for councilor James Murray. The friction within the legislature only intensified with the approach of the Revolution.[32]

In addition to serving as occasional seat of government, Bath also benefited from special legislative representation in the House of Commons. Borough representation was an extension of the institution in England wherein the particular commercial interests of towns among an overwhelmingly rural populace were accorded a voice in Parliament. Not only did that rationale obtain in North Carolina, but colonials may have envisioned borough representation as a means of encouraging the establishment and growth of urban areas. Legislation in 1715, which revived the original incorporation of Bath, granted Bath and New Bern, as well as all future towns in the province that contained at least sixty families, the right to send a single representative to the lower house of the General Assembly. Seven years later, upon the incorporation of Edenton in 1722, the legislature also accorded that town a delegate in the lower house. Edenton in 1723, and Bath and New Bern in 1731, belatedly took advantage of borough representation, and later were joined by Wilmington, whose act of incorporation in 1739/40 bestowed representation upon that town.[33]

However, as the Crown prepared to send a new governor to North Carolina in the early 1750s following the death of Governor Johnston, it noted that the erection of towns and the privilege of borough representation derived from the royal prerogative, not from statute law. Hence in 1752 three laws chartering towns, including two that bestowed the borough franchise, were disallowed, though the Bath statute of 1715 was not among them. Royal instructions to newly appointed governor Arthur Dobbs, who arrived in the colony in 1754, ordered him to establish towns and grant borough representation by royal charters, though the Crown told Dobbs to permit Bath, New Bern, Edenton, and Wilmington to continue their legislative representation. Still, since the 1715 statute had not been repealed, any town might avail itself of legislative representation once it reached the minimum of sixty resident families. Moreover, the General Assembly remained defiant, as usual, in the face of the royal prerogative, for it continued to charter towns and in the case of Brunswick endowed that town with legislative representation though it contained only twenty families. Before independence, nine towns (Bath, New Bern, Edenton, Wilmington, Brunswick, Halifax, Campbellton, Salisbury, and Hillsborough) enjoyed the right of borough representation.[34]

Local Politics

The statute of 1715 outlined the qualifications for voting in Bath. White males who were freemen, residents of the town, at least twenty-one years of age, paid taxes, and had lived in the colony at least a year before an election, were qualified to cast ballots. Legislation in 1723 restricted the franchise in Bath, Edenton, and all other borough towns to a resident owner of a saved lot (on which a house had been or would be erected), the owner of a lot tenanted by a person legally barred from the franchise, the renter of a saved lot who had paid taxes for the year prior to the election, and the owner of a saved lot whose house was vacant. The law also limited candidacy for borough representatives to freeholders of the town and owners of lots on which a habitable house had been erected who had been residents of North Carolina and the town for eighteen months prior to the election. On election day, the county provost marshal or sheriff, or his deputy, conducted the poll in conjunction with two inspectors. Voters deposited their ballots in a box. At the end of the day the sheriff counted the ballots in the presence of the inspectors, who also tallied the votes. In the case of a tie, the sheriff cast the deciding ballot.[35]

From 1731, when Bath delegates began to appear in the general assemblies, to 1775, eleven men represented the town in the colonial legislature. (Patrick Gordon was elected in 1766 but not seated.)

Table 1
Bath Representation in the Colonial Legislature[36]

Name	Term
Roger Kenyon	1731, 1734-1735
John Leahy (Lakey)	1733
Robert Turner	1738-1739, 1743
Richard Rigby	1738/9-1741
Wyriot Ormond	1743-1744, 1746, 1754-1757
Michael Coutanche	1745, 1746-1752, 1758-1761
Robert Palmer	1762
Wyriot Ormond (the younger)	1762-1765, 1770-1773
Patrick Gordon	1766 (not seated)
Peter Blinn	1766-1768
John Maule	1769
William Brown	1774-1775

Contentiousness, even fraud, characterized elections in Bath (and in other towns). The General Assembly apparently failed to sustain a challenge to Kenyon in the town's first election in 1731. But eight years later Richard Rigby successfully contested the election of Robert Turner, and the legislature awarded Bath's seat to Rigby. At that time Robert Boyd, who had supervised the election, was brought before the lower house and "mildly repremanded by . . . [the] Speaker for obliterating the Poll for Bath Town & other misdemeanours in contempt of the Priviledges of this House." The election of Turner in March 1743/44 was also annulled by the lower house, which found that the sheriff of Beaufort County had not administered the proper legal oath to voters. Following the issuance of a new writ of election, Wyriot Ormond Sr. received the support of the Bath electorate. Peter Blinn in 1762 unsuccessfully challenged the election of Wyriot Ormond Jr., but four years later his complaint of the "undue election" of Patrick Gordon found favor with the lower house, which dismissed Gordon and seated Blinn. Ormond in 1771 survived another challenge, when the legislature rejected a charge by Thomas Respess that Ormond had been improperly elected.[37]

Bath's legislative representatives participated in an ongoing series of political struggles over a period of four decades that ultimately culminated in a revolution for independence. Two years before Roger Kenyon took his seat in the General Assembly in 1731, the proprietors of North and South Carolina had sold their colonies to the Crown, but the change in ownership did little to abate the internal turmoil that had long characterized the northern province. In the vacuum created by the negligence of the proprietors, North Carolinians had developed a long legacy of self-government. The colony's partial geographic isolation—occasioned by the protective barrier of the Outer Banks, the generally lax oversight exercised by the British government, and a rapid rate of immigration by mid-century—reinforced the independent inclinations of the colonists. George Burrington, who had previously assaulted Roger Kenyon, became the first royal governor of North Carolina and coincidentally convened the legislative session to which Kenyon was elected. However, the governor retained his fearsome temper in conjunction with a foul mouth and a touch of paranoia that alienated most in the colony.[38]

The Crown replaced Burrington in 1734 with Gabriel Johnston, a Scotsman who remained governor until his death in 1752, the longest tenure of all the royal governors of North Carolina. Like Burrington, Johnston found reconciling the interests of the Crown and colonists virtually impossible. The governor quarreled with the lower house of the General Assembly over numerous issues, including his salary, fees for royal officials, the emission of paper money, and the payment of quitrents, a fixed tax on land that was imposed by the Crown. Legislation in 1735 named Bath as one of three places in Beaufort Precinct at which quitrents might be paid. Eight years later Bath became one of two locations in the county in which other taxes (provincial, county, parish) might also be paid. While colonials agreed in principle to taxation, most preferred that the provost marshal or sheriff come to their residences to collect the levies, which, of course, would have made collection far more difficult. Although Carolinians fairly dutifully paid their provincial and county taxes, the Crown realized relatively little money from quitrents. Beaufort was one of seven counties in 1772-1773 in which the royal receiver general of quitrents collected no money.[39]

In addition to the differences between the governor and the General Assembly, another sectional confrontation in the 1740s known as the "representation controversy" divided the Albemarle and southern counties (formerly the precincts of Bath County). The southern counties, including Beaufort, which were entitled to two delegates each to the lower house of the General Assembly, objected to the inordinate representation of the northern counties, which since the seventeenth century had been accorded five delegates each. Adding to the dispute was the need to establish a permanent capital for the colony instead of the peripatetic seat of government that met at Edenton, Bath, New Bern, and Wilmington. Governor Johnston, who sided with the southern interests, finally called a meeting of the legislature at Wilmington in November 1746, which the northern counties boycotted. At that session of the General Assembly, the representatives from Beaufort County and Bath, along with other southern legislators, voted to equalize representation at two per county, and to make New Bern the capital. Northerners objected, leading to eight divisive years that bordered on anarchy in the Albemarle counties. The matter was finally resolved after Johnston's death, when Arthur Dobbs, his successor, brought instructions from the Crown in 1754 to void the Wilmington proceedings, in effect returning the colony to its former method of legislative representation and leaving it again without a permanent capital, all to the dismay of the inhabitants of Bath and Beaufort County.[40]

In the meantime Bath, because of its status as a seaport, felt the impact of several inter-colonial wars that involved England and English colonials with their French and Spanish counterparts. Queen Anne's War (1702-1713), the War of Jenkins' Ear and King George's War (1739-1748), and the French and Indian War (1754-1763) found the enemy menacing North Carolina's coast, though Bath was not invaded and occupied, as were Beaufort in 1747 and Brunswick Town in 1748. From the perspective of Bath, most of the damage by the enemy in those wars was inflicted on shipping, which disrupted trade and raised marine insurance rates. In 1748 a French privateer "belonging to Cape Francois" (present Haiti) slipped inside Ocracoke Inlet and plundered the brig *Molly* of Boston, which had just left Bath, and a sloop belonging to merchant James Calef (Calife, Calf) of Bath. In 1760 the sloop *Elizabeth and Ann*, "belonging to Bath Town" and bound for the island of Tortola in the West Indies, was seized by a French privateer, taken to Cape François, and condemned as a prize.[41] Ultimately the French and Indian War concluded in 1763 with a resounding victory for the British, who ousted the French from the North American continent and seized Florida from Spain.

Moving towards Revolution

However, the end of the French and Indian War witnessed the beginning of a rift between the mother country and the colonies that ultimately led to American independence. Sensing a growing colonial independency and relieved of the need to seek colonial cooperation to defend the continent against the French and

Spanish, the British tried to strengthen their control over the colonies in America. A royal proclamation restricted westward migration, and the Crown and Parliament attempted to enforce more rigidly laws that governed colonial commerce. At the same time the British sought colonial aid in recouping the enormous costs of the war, a policy that resulted in the imposition of taxes that colonials found objectionable. Whether the Carolinians resented paying additional levies to the British government or believed that the taxes violated their rights—no taxation without representation—violent opposition met the attempted implementation of the Stamp Act in 1765 in North Carolina and throughout the colonies. Parliament repealed the obnoxious law in 1766 but followed the next year with new taxes and a determined effort to compel the colonials to abide by imperial commercial regulations.

While North Carolinians attempted to cope with the new British colonial policy, a crisis engulfed their own colony in the form of the Regulation or Regulator Movement. A massive protest principally by western settlers who harbored a number of grievances, including high taxes, corrupt public officials, and unrepresentative government, the Regulation forced Gov. William Tryon to call upon militia in the eastern counties to march into the backcountry to maintain order. An expedition in 1768, in which Robert Palmer of Bath was one of seven lieutenant generals appointed by Tryon, ended peacefully, but another in 1771 resulted in an armed confrontation—the Battle of Alamance—between the governor's forces and the Regulators. Tryon called upon Beaufort County to contribute a company of fifty men to the second expedition. Slightly fewer appeared—thirty-five rank and file, a drummer, and officers, including Capt. John Patten (Patton) and Col. Robert Palmer. In a pitched battle on May 16, 1771, Tryon's forces defeated the Regulators and broke their organization, though not their egalitarian spirit and demand for more responsive government.[42]

Soon after the Battle of Alamance, the imperial crisis again occupied the attention of North Carolinians. When the Tea Act passed by Parliament in 1773 evoked colonial opposition in the form of the Boston Tea Party, the British legislature responded with the Intolerable Acts. Although that group of laws was designed to punish Boston and Massachusetts, it aroused the ire of all the colonies. They convened a Continental Congress in 1774 to form plans to retaliate against the British, followed by a second Continental Congress in 1775 that became the governing agency for first the colonies and then the states after independence was declared in 1776.

North Carolina early became embroiled in the anti-English furor. Many in the colony, and some perhaps in Bath, remained loyal to the English government, as did Robert Palmer, who was resident in England. However, the rebels or Patriots soon took control. North Carolina held five provincial congresses between 1774 and 1776. Those congresses elected delegates to represent the colony in the continental congresses, carried out the mandates of the continental congresses, created a provisional government for the colony of North Carolina in 1775, proposed to the Second Continental Congress that the colonies declare their independence, and wrote a constitution for the independent state of North Carolina in 1776.

Merchant, postmaster, and tavern keeper William Brown, Bath's last delegate to the colonial legislature and most eminent citizen on the eve of the Revolution, represented the town in all five provincial congresses. His service was undistinguished in the first two meetings, but in the third congress in Hillsborough in 1775, Brown was appointed to committees to prepare a plan for a provisional government for the colony and to investigate the conduct of a man suspected of opposing the American cause. His committee assignments in the fourth and fifth congresses at Halifax, respectively, included settling military and naval claims and devising means "for apprehending & bringing to justice the Tories in Bladen County." The fifth congress, which drafted the state constitution of 1776, also enacted a number of ordinances to establish and maintain the independent state government until the legislature met the following year. In the process Brown was named a justice of the peace for Beaufort County and collector for the customs district of Port Bath.[43]

Brown justified the recognition, for from his home in Bath he played a vital role in bringing about the Revolution, particularly as a member of the safety committee for Beaufort County. Safety committees, authorized by the First Continental Congress, formed in the towns and counties of the colonies to carry out the directives of the congress, including economic sanctions against Great Britain and punitive measures against those who opposed the American effort. In effect, safety committees became the "engines of revolution" at the grass-roots level. When news of the clash between colonial militia and British soldiers at Lexington on April 19, 1775, arrived in Bath, Brown and Roger Ormond, as members of the safety committee, received the message and transmitted it to their counterparts in New Bern. Brown's home served as a recruitment center for North Carolina troops. William Brown and Bath contributed as well as they could to the cause of American independence.[44]

NOTES

1. Clark, *State Records*, 23:73-74.

2. Clark, *State Records*, 23:74; James R. Hoyle, "Plan of Bath Town," 1807, copied from a draft dated 1766, in Reed, *Beaufort County*, following 48; Lefler and Powell, *Colonial North Carolina*, 57; Book 1, pp. 347-348 (microfilm), Beaufort County Deeds.

3. Clark, *State Records*, 23:74; Book 2, pp. 61-62, 166-167, 172-173, 188, 196, 360-361 (microfilm), Beaufort County Deeds.

4. Clark, *State Records*, 23:75-76; Book 2, pp. 36-37 (microfilm), Beaufort County Deeds.

5. Clark, *State Records*, 23:74, 239; 25:193; Donald R. Lennon, "The Development of Town Government in Colonial North Carolina," in *Of Tar Heel Towns, Shipbuilders, Reconstructionists and Alliancemen* (Greenville, N.C.: East Carolina University Publications, Department of History, 1981), 10-11.

6. Lennon, "Development of Town Government in North Carolina," 6-8; Mary Phlegar Smith, "Borough Representation in North Carolina," *North Carolina Historical Review* 7 (April 1930): 177-191; Alan D. Watson, *Society in Colonial North Carolina*, rev. ed. (Raleigh: Division of Archives and History, Department of Cultural Resources, 1996), 120.

7. Clark, *State Records*, 23:810; 25:176, 470; Alan D. Watson, "The Town Fathers of Early Wilmington, 1743-1775," Lower Cape Fear Historical Society *Bulletin* 24 (October 1980).

8. Clark, *State Records*, 23:76, 239, 805, 810-813; 25:208, 230. Between 1715 and 1745, John Clark (Clarke), John Drinkwater, Roger Kenyon, Thomas Michael McDonagh, Henry Crofton, Robert Turner, Patrick Maule, Oliver Blackburn (Blackbourn), and Stephen Goolde, among others, served as commissioners; after 1745, Robert Boyd, Peter Blinn, and Wyriot Ormond. Book 2, pp. 60, 61-62, 107, 137, 172-173, 243, 246, 248; Book 4, p. 160 (microfilm), Beaufort County Deeds.

9. Clark, *State Records*, 23:146-149, 234-235, 304-308, 749-750, 968-969.

10. Clark, *State Records*, 23:73.

11. Clark, *State Records*, 23:74; Donald R. Lennon and Ida B. Kellam, eds., *The Wilmington Town Book, 1743-1778* (Raleigh: Division of Archives and History, Department of Cultural Resources, 1973), 222, 223, 226, 227, 229, 230-231, 232, and passim.

12. Clark, *State Records*, 23:115, 239.

13. Clark, *State Records*, 23:74; 25:191-192; Lennon and Kellam, *Wilmington Town Book*, 56, 161-162, 199, 210, 214, 232-233, 236-237, 238; Watson, *History of New Bern and Craven County*, 52.

14. Clark, *State Records*, 23:138-139, 232-233, 238, 304-308, 454, 466; C. J. Sauthier maps of Edenton, New Bern, and Bath, 1769, State Archives, Office of Archives and History, Raleigh; Lennon, "Development of Town Government in Colonial North Carolina," 15. The 1807 map of Bath shows the northern boundary designated by a ditch and a town gate on King Street.

15. Clark, *State Records*, 23:150, 239; Minutes of the Beaufort County Court of Pleas and Quarter Sessions, September term 1761, State Archives, Office of Archives and History, Raleigh.

16. Clark, *State Records*, 23:74-75, 100-102; Paschal, *History of Colonial Bath*, 38.

17. Clark, *State Records*, 23:100-102; 25:192-193; Paschal, *History of Colonial Bath*, 38.

18. Colonial Court Records, General Court, Criminal Papers, 1730-1734, State Archives, Office of Archives and History, Raleigh.

19. Clark, *State Records*, 25:329; Beaufort County Court Minutes, September term 1756.

20. Clark, *State Records*, 25:343; Beaufort County Court Minutes, June, September, and December terms 1756.

21. Clark, *State Records*, 23:531, 533, 680-681; Beaufort County Court Minutes, March and June terms 1761; Reed, *Beaufort County*, 103-109; William S. Powell, ed., *The North Carolina Gazetteer* (Chapel Hill: University of North Carolina Press, 1968), 518.

22. C. J. Sauthier Map of Bath, 1769; Reed, *Beaufort County*, 55. A limited-scope exploration held on this lot by East Carolina University archaeologists in the summer of 2002 failed to locate any traces of the courthouse or jail.

23. Clark, *State Records*, 23:100-102; Robert J. Cain, ed., *North Carolina Higher-Court Records, 1724-1730*, vol. 6 of *The Colonial Records of North Carolina [Second Series]* (Raleigh: Division of Archives and History, Department of Cultural Resources, 1981), 174.

24. Paul M. McCain, *The County Court in North Carolina before 1750* (Durham, N.C.: Duke University Press, 1954).

25. Beaufort County Court Minutes, March term 1757, March term 1758, March term 1759, September term 1761; Alan D. Watson, "The Constable in Colonial North Carolina," *North Carolina Historical Review* 68 (January 1991): 4-7.

26. Watson, "Constable in Colonial North Carolina," 10-11, 13-14.

27. Lennon and Kellam, *Wilmington Town Book*, 25, 28, 41, 47, 55, 58, 65, 66, 71, 84, 97, 106, 112, 123-124, 177, 185, 214, 219; Watson, "Constable in Colonial North Carolina," 15-16.

28. William S. Price Jr., "'Men of Good Estate': Wealth among North Carolina Royal Councillors," *North Carolina Historical Review* 49 (winter 1972): 72-82.

29. Robert J. Cain, ed., *Records of the Executive Council, 1735-1754*, vol. 8 of *The Colonial Records of North Carolina [Second Series]* (Raleigh: Division of Archives and History, Department of Cultural Resources, 1988), 43-44, 155-175, 196-200, 281-295.

30. Saunders, *Colonial Records*, 4:714-732.

31. Saunders, *Colonial Records*, 4:714-716, 732; Jack P. Greene, *The Quest for Power: The Lower Houses of Assembly in the Southern Royal Colonies, 1689-1776* (Chapel Hill: University of North Carolina Press, 1963), 440-441.

32. Saunders, *Colonial Records*, 4:1317-1348; Clark, *State Records*, 23:371-386; 25:248-249.

33. Clark, *State Records*, 23:79; 25:178; John L. Cheney Jr., *North Carolina Government: A Narrative and Statistical History, 1585-1979* (Raleigh: North Carolina Department of the Secretary of State, 1981), 33, 36; Smith, "Borough Representation in North Carolina," 177-180; Herbert R. Paschal Jr., "Proprietary North Carolina: A Study in Colonial Government" (Ph.D. diss., University of North Carolina, 1961), 626-627.

34. Smith, "Borough Representation in North Carolina," 177-180.

35. Clark, *State Records*, 23:12-14; 25:191; Smith, "Borough Representation in North Carolina," 181-183.

36. Cheney, *North Carolina Government*, 89 nn. 100, 101; 90 nn. 128, 129; 1057.

37. Saunders, *Colonial Records*, 3:289; 4:384, 389, 653; 6:897; 7:350, 352; 8:317, 441; Cheney, *North Carolina Government*, 88 nn. 43, 44; 89 nn. 100, 101; 90 nn. 128, 129; 91 nn. 174, 175.

38. William S. Price Jr., "A Strange Incident in George Burrington's Governorship," *North Carolina Historical Review* 51 (spring 1974): 149-158.

39. Clark, *State Records*, 23:212-213; 25:217; Saunders, *Colonial Records*, 9:608-610.

40. Lawrence F. London, "The Representation Controversy in North Carolina," *North Carolina Historical Review* 11 (October 1934): 255-270; A. Roger Ekirch, *"Poor Carolina": Politics and Society in Colonial North Carolina, 1729-1776* (Chapel Hill: University of North Carolina Press, 1981), 86-111.

41. Book 2, p. 522 (microfilm), Beaufort County Deeds; Saunders, *Colonial Records*, 6:239-240.

42. Saunders, *Colonial Records*, 8:574, 582-594 passim, 670, 677, 697, 702; William S. Powell, James K. Huhta, and Thomas J. Farnham, eds., *The Regulators in North Carolina: A Documentary History, 1759-1776* (Raleigh: State Department of Archives and History, 1971), 461, 590.

43. Saunders, *Colonial Records*, 9:1041-1043, 1049, 1178-1181; 10:164-169, 172-175, 499-501, 504, 522-523, 913-915, 935-936; Clark, *State Records*, 23:987-988, 992.

44. Saunders, *Colonial Records*, 9:1236-1237; 10:646; Clark, *State Records*, 11:355, 805-806; Alan D. Watson, "The Committees of Safety and the Coming of the American Revolution in North Carolina, 1774-1776," *North Carolina Historical Review* 73 (April 1996): 131-155.

3

Economy

Although few in number and modest in size, towns played a critical role in the economic development of the North Carolina colony. While the advantages touted by the proprietors for towns were many, urban areas, however small, served principally as commercial centers, and Bath was no exception. Port towns, like Bath, acted as conduits for external trade, providing the facilities for exporting provincial goods and for importing necessary or desirable foreign products. Towns remained small because they were little more than transshipment points (in addition to centers of government). Thus their size did not necessarily reflect their volume of commerce or importance.

Bath, no doubt, was purposely located to take advantage of the shipping potential of Ocracoke Inlet. Punctuating the barrier islands along North Carolina's extensive coastline—the Outer Banks or Banks—were numerous inlets that linked the Atlantic Ocean to the colony's sounds. While inlets between the Virginia line and Cape Lookout appeared and closed over the years, often as the result of hurricanes, as many as twenty-five remained open long enough to acquire names and appear on maps. The most important for commercial purposes before the Revolution were Old and New Currituck, Roanoke, and Ocracoke. Below Cape Lookout to Cape Fear, Beaufort (Old Topsail), Bogue, Bear, New River, and New Inlets offered the best access to interior waters.[1]

Because North Carolina was first settled by Virginians who extended their southern frontier into the Albemarle region, Currituck and Roanoke Inlets assumed the most immediate importance for trade. Old Currituck Inlet, closed by 1731, was replaced by New Currituck, which opened about five miles to the south in the wake of a storm in 1713. However, both inlets were shallow, which limited trade to small coastal craft and rendered shipping activity on Currituck Sound inconsequential during the colonial era. Roanoke Inlet, located at the eastern end of Albemarle Sound, was ideal for the trade of the northeastern corner of North Carolina, but its lack of depth also restricted its use to vessels of small burden. Moreover, according to Gov. George Burrington in 1731, "Roanoke is so dangerous that few people care to use it but go round to Ocacock."[2]

As the population of North Carolina spread into the Pamlico region, Ocracoke Inlet, linking Pamlico Sound and the Atlantic Ocean, became North Carolina's principal avenue to the outside world. Burrington claimed that Ocracoke Inlet was "the only place that has a sufficient depth of water for a ship of Burden between Topsail (Beaufort) and the Capes of Virginia." Yet the inlet had its drawbacks. Its channels or sluices were still so shallow that larger ships had to lighter, or unload cargo offshore; it lacked a protected harbor, leaving vessels riding at the mercy of an often-harsh sea; and it opened to a dangerous coastline between Cape Hatteras and Cape Lookout. Nevertheless, the greater utility of Ocracoke Inlet must have influenced the decision of the founders of Bath to locate their town near one of the principal rivers feeding into Pamlico Sound and in proximity to the inlet. Sheltered along Bath Creek about twenty-one miles from the mouth of Pamlico River, Bath lay fifty-five miles from Ocracoke Inlet.[3]

Port Bath

The town of Bath assumed an importance beyond that of its status as a port when it became the seat of the customs district known as Port Bath. Almost a half century after its first permanent settlement in America, the English government instituted a policy to regulate the commerce of its burgeoning empire. That effort, beginning in the Cromwellian era but pursued more vigorously upon the restoration of the Stuarts in 1660, was embodied in a series of parliamentary statutes called Navigation Acts. Dominated by mercantilist conceptions that emphasized the importance of trade for national prosperity and military superiority, the English sought by the navigation legislation to direct colonial commerce so that it might best serve and sustain the empire, and particularly the mother country.

In order to properly regulate shipping, the English created customs districts with designated ports of entry in the various American colonies. By 1710 there were thirty-four customs districts from Newfoundland to the Carolinas, including the Bahamas and Bermuda. While most colonies merited one or two districts, the long coastlines and absence of coastal towns in Maryland and Virginia required nine and ten districts, respectively. A half century later, in 1760, the total number of districts had risen to forty-five, including five in North Carolina.[4]

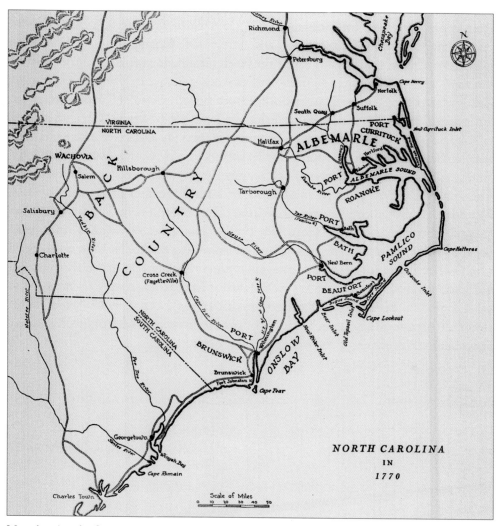

Map showing the five customs districts in North Carolina in 1770. From Charles Christopher Crittenden, *The Commerce of North Carolina, 1763-1789* (New Haven: Yale University Press, 1936), 196.

During the first fifty years of North Carolina's existence, when settlement was confined mainly to the Albemarle region, two customs districts sufficed for the colony. Port Currituck included the area of Currituck Sound; Port Roanoke, with Edenton as its port of entry, encompassed the Albemarle Sound. As the colony expanded southward, Ports Bath, Beaufort, and Brunswick were established. In 1716 the proprietors acceded to a request from residents of Bath Town and Bath County to designate the town a "Sea Port Town." Eventually, the customs district of Port Bath was established, and Bath Town became an official port of entry. The district encompassed Ocracoke Inlet, Pamlico Sound, and the rivers, including the Neuse, which fed into the sound. Port Beaufort appeared in the wake of the incorporation of the town of Beaufort in 1722, and New Bern and the Neuse River were placed in that jurisdiction in 1730. As early as March 1731, probably originating with the appointment and arrival of George Burrington, North Carolina's first royal governor, Port Brunswick became the official port of entry for the Cape Fear region.[5]

Customs officials appointed by the Treasury Board in England administered the customs districts and were usually seated at the ports of entry. At a fully staffed port, such as New York, the customs list carried a surveyor and searcher, a collector, a comptroller, and such minor functionaries as tidewaiters and landwaiters. Only the largest ports warranted a surveyor and searcher, who was primarily responsible for the actual inspection of ships and control of harbor facilities. For most ports the collector was the preeminent customs officer. Upon him fell the full responsibility for enforcing the Navigation Acts—the proper loading and unloading of cargoes, collecting the payment of duties, and transmitting accounts and receipts to England. The comptroller had the negative function of checking the affairs of the collector, though in practice his office was often reduced to the status of a subordinate to the collector. Tidewaiters, often hired on a daily or "need" basis, were put on board incoming vessels to prevent clandestine landings of cargoes; landwaiters took charge at the wharves.[6]

Table 2

Customs Collectors for Port Bath in the Eighteenth Century

Customs Collector	Dates Served	Remarks
William Alexander	To 1724	Also served as comptroller for Port Currituck
Isaac Ottiwell	March 1724-1731	Deceased while in office
William Owen	December 1731-1735	Deceased while in office
Roger Ormond	June 1735-1736	Deceased while in office
John Rieusset	July 1736-1739	Deceased while in office
George Gould	January 1739-1753?	Deceased while in office, sometime between 1749 and 1753
Robert Palmer	June 1753-1772	Resigned because of poor health
William Palmer	February 1772-1776	Last royal appointee
William Brown	December 1776-1777	Collector of Continental Impost. Appointed by North Carolina General Assembly
Nathan Keais	1777-1790? (at least)	Collector of Continental Impost

SOURCE: Wilson Angley, "Port Bath, North Carolina, in the Eighteenth Century: A Compilation of Records" (report, Research Branch, Division of Archives and History, Raleigh, 1981), 42-46; Saunders, *Colonial Records*, 5:36; 9:323.

Although technically not part of the customs establishment, the naval officer early played an integral role in customs affairs by recording incoming and outgoing ships and validating performance bonds offered by ships' captains. First appointed by the colonial governors but increasingly responsible to the home government, the naval officer eventually emerged as a record-keeping subsidiary to the customs officials. Rather than provide yet another restraint upon the collector in accordance with the English enthusiasm for checks and cross checks, the naval officer became an additional enforcement agent, though at no expense to the customs establishment. Scattered references to the naval officer at Port Bath indicate that Stephen Go(u)ld occupied that position in 1731.[7]

Port Bath, like many of the American districts, ordinarily lost money, for customs receipts seldom covered expenses. In the fiscal year ending October 10, 1767, revenue obtained from duties on the importation of sugar, molasses, and coffee, imposed in compliance with the Molasses and Sugar Acts of 1733 and 1764, respectively, amounted to £19.11.7½. Expenses incurred for the salary of the collector, £40, the hire of boats and men, £10, stationery, £20, postage, £1.3.9, and office rent, £10, totaled £81.3.9, created an operating deficit of £61.12.1½. By way of comparison, Port Brunswick received £88.12.8 in revenue, incurred £166.19.2 in expenses, and lost £78.6.6. The even greater volume of trade conducted in Charleston, South Carolina, was reflected in receipts of £4,079.13.0 and expenses of £362.2.8, for a net profit of £3,717.10.4.[8]

In order to facilitate maritime trade to Port Bath, the General Assembly in 1723 named five self-perpetuating commissioners to administer the port—Maurice Moore, John Porter, John Baptista Ashe, Thomas Boyd, and Patrick Maule—and authorized them to use the powder and lead money (a levy in kind on each vessel entering the customs district) collected during the ensuing year to erect buoys and beacons to mark the Swash and other channels in Ocracoke Inlet and the sea lane from the inlet to Bath. The legislature reiterated that policy in 1739 when it appointed commissioners of navigation and pilotage (whom the governor might replace) for each customs district in the colony, and directed the commissioners to use the powder money (without a time limitation) to hire persons to delineate the routes from Edenton, Bath, and New Bern to Ocracoke Inlet. The legislation also instructed the commissioners to mark the Swash and other channels in the inlet. Moreover, they were to "find and Provide two good and Sufficient sailing Boats" for the benefit of pilots, who would be recommended by the commissioners to the governor for licensing. Thereafter the pilots were expected to bring ships through Ocracoke Inlet to the respective inland ports, to maintain the buoys and beacons, and to report any alterations in the channels.[9]

A succession of statutes throughout the remainder of the colonial era repeated and refined the 1739 enactment. Legislation in 1752 named new commissioners for each port district (Michael Coutanche, Samuel Sinclare, and James Calef [Calf] for Port Bath), making them self-perpetuating. Rather than using powder money to raise funds for staking and marking the channels at Ocracoke Inlet and to the respective ports, a tonnage duty was imposed on ships entering the districts. The commissioners were authorized to recommend pilots for their respective districts to the governor for his appointment. The law also established a fee schedule for pilots who thereafter would be paid by ships' captains for their services. By 1759, declining trade to Port Bath rendered the tonnage duty insufficient for the district, so the General Assembly instructed the commissioners to sell the accumulated surplus of powder and lead (though reserving a sufficient supply for the proposed Fort Granville at Ocracoke), and use the proceeds to defray the costs of navigation improvements. The duties of the commissioners of navigation and pilotage (Robert Palmer, Thomas Respess, Wyriot Ormond, and Peter Blinn for Port Bath in 1766) remained unchanged until the Revolution.[10]

The General Assembly also attempted to improve the quality of exports from North Carolina and thereby enhance commerce by establishing an inspection system to regulate the packing and shipping of goods leaving the province. Legislation in 1715 addressed pork, beef, pitch, and tar. Later, beginning in the 1750s, additional commodities were added to the inspection list, including hemp, flax, flaxseed, rice, flour, butter, turpentine, indigo, tanned leather, deerskins, staves, shingles, headings, and lumber. At the same time separate laws instituted an elaborate inspection system for tobacco exports. The statutes fixed inspection sites in the counties and appointed or required county courts to appoint inspectors.[11]

Bath served as one of the inspection sites in Beaufort County, largely because it was the seat of the customs district. Moreover, the town possessed a convenient warehouse after 1743. In that year the legislature decided that the public warehouse that had been erected at Core Point on the south bank of the Pamlico River for the purpose of housing the commodities that county residents used to pay their taxes in kind was "very inconvenient to the Inhabitants of the . . . County." It ordered the Beaufort County Court to replace the Core Point warehouse with structures at Bath and at Red Banks on the Pamlico River. Subsequently the warehouse in Bath was used for export inspections as well. When not needed for inspection purposes, the warehouse was rented or used to keep the levy of powder and lead paid by ship captains to the collector of customs at Port Bath.[12]

Bath's Exports — Agricultural and Timber Products and Naval Stores

Shipping constituted the lifeline of North Carolina's external trade, though overland commerce with neighboring colonies was also consequential. However, most Carolinians labored in the fields and forests, as attested by the exports of Port Bath. The colonials overwhelmingly turned to agriculture, for land provided subsistence as well as commodities for sale. Most farmers grew mainly what they needed for household purposes. Where they had access to markets, usually by water, some farmers with sufficient labor and capital were tempted to produce surpluses for sale beyond their immediate locale. In the vicinity of Bath, where several prominent town residents owned plantations, including Thomas Harding, Roger Kenyon, John Rieusset, Edward Howcott (Houit, Howcut), Michael Coutanche, and Robert Palmer, corn proved the most valuable of the non-animal foodstuffs, accompanied by insignificant amounts of potatoes and beans.

Most colonials raised livestock, and some possessed prodigious herds of hogs and cattle, which they often loosed in the woods to forage. The export of hogs and cattle, either salted or on the hoof, indicated the importance of that element of agriculture for those living in the Bath shipping district. The animal byproducts of lard and tallow also appeared in a number of shipments from Bath. North Carolinians reportedly prided themselves on having the largest flocks of domestic poultry or barnyard fowl in the English empire, but rarely did those animals appear on the shipping lists. Many farmers kept stocks of bees for honey and wax, but relatively little of either was shipped from North Carolina.[13]

North Carolina farmers grew tobacco, wheat, rice, and indigo, often for export. The tobacco culture was early confined to the Albemarle region, but it spread into the inner Coastal Plain in the eighteenth century. Although grown along the lower and upper reaches of the Tar-Pamlico River by the 1750s, tobacco is rarely mentioned in extant shipping records for Port Bath. Wheat, also early grown for export in the Albemarle, later shifted to the backcountry where resident Germans preferred it to corn. The Lower Cape Fear produced almost all of the rice and indigo shipped from North Carolina, for those were labor- and capital-intensive crops that could only be undertaken for profit by the wealthy slave-owning planters in the area. An occasional shipment of rice made its way through Port Bath, probably indicative of experimentation with that grain along the Tar-Pamlico and its tributaries. Colonials grew small amounts of cotton, mostly for household purposes, though three casks of the fiber were shipped through Port Bath to Annapolis, Maryland, in 1764.[14]

North Carolinians also turned to their abundant forests to produce a variety of wood products, particularly sawn lumber (boards, plank, scantling), shingles, and staves. The sawn lumber was cut in the colony's numerous sawmills. John Lawson

Sketch of a colonial turpentine distillery in the forest. From Frederick Law Olmsted, *A Journey in the Seaboard Slaves States; With Remarks on their Economy* (London: Sampson Low, Son, and Co., 1856), 344.

noted that the "white and yellow Pines are saw'd into Planks for several Uses. They make Masts, Yards, and a great many other Necessaries therewith, the Pine being the most useful Tree in the Woods." Colonials laboriously fashioned shingles and staves by hand. They made the former mainly from white cedar and cypress trees, pliable wood found throughout the swamps and lowlands of the Coastal Plain. Staves, like shingles, were made from durable, resistant woods, especially white oak and red (now probably called black) oak, which also grew abundantly in the bottomlands along the coast. Pipe staves, barrel staves, and hogshead staves were shaped and measured according to their intended purpose. Other wood products included heading (the tops of casks and barrels), posts, oars, spars, and house frames.[15]

Among the eastern seaboard colonies, North Carolina was England's largest supplier of naval stores on the eve of the Revolution. Since 1705, the colony had enjoyed a Parliamentary bounty on the products that was designed to encourage exportation. Naval stores, variously defined but principally consisting of turpentine, rosin, tar, and pitch, derived from the longleaf pines found in eastern North Carolina. Lawson had recognized the potential of the "Pitch-Pine . . . [that]

affords the four great Necessaries, Pitch, Tar, Rozin, and Turpentine." The colonials obtained crude, or common, turpentine by "boxing" living trees. The process involved stripping the bark from a portion of the trunk and making incisions in the area. The heat of the spring and summer months drew the rosin from the tree down the incisions into wooden receptacles. Refining crude turpentine produced distilled or spirits of turpentine, the residue of which was rosin. Approximately ten barrels of crude turpentine yielded one barrel of spirits of turpentine. Spirits of turpentine was a component of paints and medicine, a solvent, and a fuel for lamps; rosin served to waterproof leather and mixed with lard and lye to make soap.[16]

The production of tar, which was rosin obtained from pinewood, and pitch required greater effort. A kiln consisting of a circular floor of clay perhaps thirty feet in diameter was prepared into which was piled split deadwood pine to a height of some fourteen feet. A pipe of wood or a ditch in the ground extended from the center to about ten feet beyond the edge of the kiln. The pile was covered with earth except for a hole in the center through which the wood inside was set on fire. At that time the opening was sealed. The resulting heat, regulated by punching sticks through the earthen cover to provide air to the interior, forced the rosin from the deadwood into the pipe or ditch at the end of which was a barrel to collect the substance called tar. Boiling tar in large iron kettles or holes in the ground lined with clay produced pitch. Three barrels of tar yielded one to two barrels of pitch. The colonials used tar to protect roofs of houses from the elements and rope from the corrosive effects of salt water, and pitch to coat the hulls of ships. When Bath residents requested that their town be designated a seaport, they pointed out that not only was the town "the most proper place within the . . .. Province for ships to take in Masts, Pitch Tar Turpentine and other Naval Stores," but also that "great Tracts of Land lye contiguous to . . . Bath Town which may afford great quantities of Naval Stores."[17]

Despite the optimistic forecast of Bath's importance as an export center for naval stores, Port Bath ranked fourth among North Carolina's five shipping districts in the export of the pine derivatives. Between 1768 and 1771, about 75 percent of the colony's naval stores exited Ports Brunswick and Beaufort, 17 to 20 percent from Port Roanoke, and 5 to 10 percent from Port Bath. Exports from Port Currituck were negligible. Nevertheless, naval stores figured prominently in Port Bath's trade. Using a sample of 129 ships that cleared Port Brunswick between 1749 and 1768, 120, or 93 percent, carried one or more naval stores products.[18]

Exports of wood products ranked second only to naval stores in colonial North Carolina. The colony annually accounted for about one-twelfth to one-fifteenth of the sawn lumber shipped from the North American provinces to Britain, about one-seventh to one-eighth of the shingles, and about one-tenth to one-twelfth of the staves. Of North Carolina's shipping districts, Port Bath ranked a distant second behind Port Brunswick in the exportation of sawn lumber, last or next to last in shingles, and next to last in staves. In the above-cited sample of 129 ships clearing Port Brunswick between 1749 and 1768, only 29 percent transported wood products. Among them was the schooner *Dispatch*, which took 1,900 feet of plank, 3,516 feet of oak boards, 1,400 hogshead staves, 6,000 hogshead headings, and 1,220 shingles to Jamaica in 1765.[19]

Hides and skins, foodstuffs, and animal products also constituted prominent exports. The trade in hides and skins dominated the Bath County economy at the beginning of the eighteenth century and continued to play a major role up to the Revolution. Forty-one percent of the sample of 129 vessels leaving Port Bath between 1749 and 1768 contained cargoes described variously as deerskins, leather, hides ("raw" and tanned), furs, and raccoon skins. Thirty-nine percent of the ships carried foodstuffs, among which pork and beef were the most prominent, although corn, beans, peas, rice, bread, flour, potatoes, and fish added variety to the trade. Occasionally livestock was shipped on the hoof: thirty hogs on the schooner *Sea Flower* in 1759; ten hogs on the sloop *Greyhound* in 1764; and livestock and two hundred fowl on the sloop *Mary* in 1765. Animal products included tallow (sixteen barrels on the sloop *Polly* in 1768) and lard, which figured in 16 and 4 percent of the 129 outward-bound voyages, respectively.[20]

Of course myriad minor items also figured in the export trade. The sloop *Goodwill* took six cannon and forty pieces of British sailcloth to Boston in 1761; the sloop *Speedwell*, eight hundred bricks and two hundred bushels of salt to Boston in 1762; the sloop *Ranger*, a desk and bookcase to Jamaica in 1763; the sloop *Hitty*, six dozen weeding hoes to Boston in 1764; and the sloop *Elizabeth*, two cables, one hawser, and one box of shoes to Boston in 1765. Four ships carried snakeroot (any of a number of plants whose roots were believed to cure snakebite) to Boston in 1765.[21]

British customs records for Port Bath from 1768 through 1772 bear out the earlier, more impressionistic accounts. Exports to Great Britain, although few, consisted almost entirely of pitch, tar, staves, and heading. More important was the traffic to the West Indies that featured wood products—boards (an annual average of 489,669 board feet), shingles, staves, and hoops; and foodstuffs—peas, corn (an annual average of 2,245 bushels), barrelled beef and pork, potatoes, and dried and pickled fish. Less important were livestock—horses, cattle, hogs, sheep, and poultry (247 dozen in 1772); and animal byproducts—tallow and lard (an annual average of 2,200 pounds). Exports to the continental colonies resembled closely those to the West Indies. Naval stores and wood products, principally staves, were prominent along with hides, deerskins, and furs (beaver, raccoon, otter, and mink). Foodstuffs, mainly corn, and animal byproducts, including an average of 1,421 pounds of beeswax from 1768 through 1771, rounded out the most significant exports.[22]

Most captains sought an assortment of goods, trying to utilize fully the capacity of their vessels to maximize profits. The sloop *Speedwell* in 1761 took naval stores, meat, staves, 200 hides, 200 deerskins, and 200 bushels of potatoes to Boston. In 1763 the brig *Bath Packett* transported 56 barrels of tar, 59 barrels of pitch, 14,400 staves, 13,600 feet of boards, 19,000 shingles, 1,000 feet of oars, 16 dozen hand spikes, 9,250 headings, 250 pine boards, 8,000 shingles, and 60 bars of iron to Kingston, Jamaica. The schooner *Unity* in 1764 shipped one bundle of deerskins, three dozen furs, four barrels of salt fish, naval stores, hides, pork, tallow, and beeswax to Annapolis. Few captains confined their cargoes to a single item, and in those cases the goods invariably consisted of naval stores.[23]

Trade Routes

Ships clearing Port Bath sailed to ports throughout the western world. Overseas, they stopped at Morocco on the Mediterranean, called at France on the European continent, docked in Greenock, Scotland, and anchored in Bristol, Liverpool, London, and Plymouth in England. Ships from Port Bath also journeyed to Honduras on the Central American coast and to myriad Caribbean destinations.[24] But the export trade of Port Bath was oriented towards the continental colonies and the West Indies, as seen in Table 3. From 1768 through 1772, only 8 vessels, or 3 percent of the total, departed for Great Britain. Another 108, or 39 percent, left for the West Indies. Of course the overseas passages required larger ships. Hence the voyages to Great Britain represented 7 percent of the total export shipping tonnage; those to the West Indies, 45 percent.

The outward-bound trade of Port Bath favored the continental colonies and the West Indies. From 1768 through 1772, 159 vessels constituting 58 percent of the ships and 47 percent of the export tonnage sailed to those destinations. Table 4 shows that Port Bath maintained a small but steady commerce with Rhode Island, New York, Pennsylvania, and Bermuda, but enjoyed a special affinity for Massachusetts, principally Boston, to which 84 voyages were made, comprising over half of the continental sailings and 31 percent of the total outward-bound ships. Boston merchants used Bath merchants as factors and left powers of attorney with Bath residents. Michael Coutanche, a native of the Channel Islands who relocated from Boston to Bath in the late 1730s, was an important figure in Bath's naval stores trade.

Table 3
Destination of Ships Clearing Port Bath, 1768-1772

Year	Great Britain		West Indies		Continental Colonies		Total	
	Number of Vessels	Total Tonnage	Number of Vessels	Total Tonnage	Number of Vessels	Total Tonnage	Number of Vessels	Total Tonnage
1768	1	130	25	1,140	24	888	50	2,158
1769	1	90	14	715	27	804	42	1,609
1770	2	260	21	996	21	652	44	1,908
1771	1	80	22	1,133	44	1,399	67	2,612
1772	3	220	26	871	43	1,332	72	2,423
Total	8	780	108	4,855	159	5,075	275	10,710

SOURCE: Ledger of Imports and Exports, British North American Ports, 1768-1773, Customs, 16/1, British Public Record Office, Photocopies, Southern Historical Collection, Chapel Hill.

Table 4
Destinations of Ships Clearing Port Bath for Continental Colonies, 1768-1772

	Newfoundland	Mass.	N.H.	Conn.	R.I.	N.Y.	Pa.	Md.	Va.
1768		13				1	5	3	
1769		13			5	2	1	1	3
1770		12			3			1	2
1771		23	1	2	5	3	2	1	4
1772	1	23		1	4	6	4	1	

	N.C.	S.C.	E. Fla.	W. Fla.	Bermuda	Total
1768					2	24
1769					3	27
1770					3	21
1771			1	1	1	44
1772	1				2	43

SOURCE: *See* Table 3.

Imports to Port Bath and the town of Bath emanated principally from the northern colonies and the West Indies. Only five, or 2 percent, of the vessels entering the district from 1768 through 1772 came from Great Britain (*see* Table 5).

More important were inbound voyages from the British and foreign West Indian islands that constituted sixty-four, or 25 percent, of the total during those years. The West Indies trade featured rum, molasses, salt, and occasionally sugar. Representative of this trade were the sloop *Providence* in 1754, which brought sugar, molasses, and rum from Kingston to Port Bath; the brig *Campbell* with sixteen slaves from Kingston in 1755; the sloop *Virgin* with three casks of sugar and four puncheons of rum in 1765 from Kingston; and the schooner *Newburn* with rum and molasses in 1767 from Kingston. Frequently vessels sailing to North Carolina failed to carry a full cargo or came in ballast, like the brig *Peggy Tryon* and the schooner *Sally*, both of which cleared Kingston in 1768 probably bound for Port Bath.[25]

Table 5
Origin and Tonnage of Ships Entering Port Bath, 1768-1772

Year	Great Britain		West Indies		Continental Colonies		Total	
	Number of Vessels	Total Tonnage	Number of Vessels	Total Tonnage	Number of Vessels	Total Tonnage	Number of Vessels	Total Tonnage
1768	1	130	10	575	29	1,113	40	1,818
1769			14	690	25	844	39	1,534
1770	1	160	6	295	34	1,131	41	1,586
1771	1	150	17	825	45	1,532	63	2,507
1772	2	170	17	622	51	1,696	70	2,488

SOURCE: *See* Table 3.

Table 6
Origin of Ships Entering Port Bath from Continental Colonies, 1768-1772

	Mass.	Conn.	R.I.	N.Y.	Pa.	Md.	Va.	N.C.	S.C.	Ga.	Bermuda	Total
1768	19	2		1	4	1	1				1	29
1769	10	2	5		1	2		2	1		2	25
1770	19		11		1	2					1	34
1771	27	4	4	1	3		3	1	1		1	45
1772	27	1	6	9	3		1		3		1	51

SOURCE: *See* Table 3.

As indicated by the above examples of the West Indies commerce, spirituous liquors constituted a large segment of Port Bath's import trade. In fact, as early as 1735 the General Assembly began to levy a tariff on such imports to augment the general revenues of the colony and on occasion to underwrite specific expenditures, such as printing the province's statutes and building Tryon Palace in New Bern. From September 16, 1761, through September 5, 1769, 162 vessels entered Port Bath carrying dutiable liquors—41,848 gallons of rum, including 2,800 gallons on the sloop *Virgin* in 1763, and 28 gallons of wine. According to Gov. William Tryon in 1767, the money obtained from the imposts on spirituous liquors was not only substantial but also "the only revenue the public can depend upon [with] any degree of punctuality in point of payment."[26]

The preponderance of Port Bath's import trade, both in terms of ships and tonnage, was conducted with the mainland colonies and Bermuda. As seen in Tables 3 and 4, from 1768 through 1772, 73 percent of the ships entering the district, representing 63 percent of the total tonnage, arrived from those destinations. Only a few voyages involved the southern colonies and Bermuda, however; most of the commerce originated in Pennsylvania, New York, and New England, particularly Massachusetts, from which 55 percent of the continental (and 40 percent of the total) vessels came. Especially prominent in the import trade were salt, an average of 2,980 bushels per year; molasses, an average of 7,099 gallons per year; and rum, an average of 5,675 gallons per year; as well as brown and loaf sugar, cheese, and flax. Additionally, foodstuffs, including dried and pickled fish, potatoes, apples, oranges, onions, and chocolate, were popular. Otherwise, 974 axes and adzes, 21,300 bricks and tiles, 404 chairs, 39 desks, and 25 tables reached the district, as did hay, cordage, iron bars, cast iron, fish oil, earthenware, woodenware, sieves, shoes, pails, a plow, 5 saddles, 48 grindstones, 2 gravestones, and 10,000 yards of straw plait.[27]

Vessels calling at North Carolina ports included ships, snows, brigs, schooners, and sloops. The full-rigged ships and snows (three-master, square-rigged craft), however, drew so much water that they had difficulty navigating the inlets and sounds along the coast. Hence they were mostly confined to North Carolina's principal deepwater port, Brunswick. The smaller brigs, equipped with two masts, a foremast with square sails and a main mast partly square- and partly fore-and-aft rigged, called infrequently at Port Bath. Most of the district's commerce, like that of North Carolina generally, was conducted in relatively small schooners and sloops. The schooner was two-masted with main and fore sails suspended by gaffs; the sloop, one-masted, fore-and-aft rigged.[28]

A sampling of the maritime records outlining the trade of Port Bath reveals an overwhelming preponderance of sloops, followed by schooners and, distantly, brigs.

Utilizing the above-cited sample of 129 vessels, but reducing the total to 101 to eliminate multiple voyages by the same ship, sloops constituted 71 of the vessels bonded at and clearing Port Bath, schooners, 25, and brigs, 5. Sloops ranged in size from 5 to 80 tons; schooners, 10 to 65; and brigs, 25 to 80. All carried crews numbering from 3 to 6 depending upon the size of the craft. Of 162 vessels paying duties on spirituous liquors in Port Bath from September 1761 to September 1769, the rigging of 140 could be identified. Of that number, 84 or 60 percent were sloops, 48 or 34 percent were schooners, 7 or 5 percent were brigs, and 1 or 1 percent was a snow. Large vessels occasionally called at Port Bath as indicated by the presence of the snow, and evidence strongly indicates that the 120-ton *Draper* of Liverpool, England, visited the district in 1751.[29]

British customs records for the years 1768 through 1772 support the contention that small vessels, principally sloops and schooners, called at Port Bath. Of the 253 ships entering the district, 234, or 92 percent, were sloops and schooners. All 5 entrances from Great Britain were larger vessels, along with 9 of 64 from the West Indies, and 5 of 184 from the Continent. Of those leaving Port Bath, 250 of 275, or 91 percent, were sloops and schooners. All 8 destined for Great Britain, 16 of 108 sailing to the West Indies, and 1 of 159 going to continental ports fell into the ship, snow, or brig categories. Indicative of the shallow waters of the northeastern corner of the colony, all but 2 of the 246 vessels entering Port Currituck and all 221 clearing that port from 1768 through 1772 were sloops and schooners. By contrast, at Port Brunswick, sloops and schooners constituted only 49 percent (317 of 641) of entrances and 47 percent (297 of 626) of clearances, confirming that district's distinction as North Carolina's principal deepwater port.[30]

Several vessels in the Port Bath trade originated in Bath. Although not a major industry in North Carolina, shipbuilding was undertaken throughout the coastal area from the Albemarle to the Cape Fear. Shipwright and town commissioner Thomas Harding doubtlessly was responsible for many of the early craft built in the vicinity of Bath, including the first recorded ship built in the Pamlico area. In 1710 Governor Cary contracted with Harding to build at his landing on Bath Creek a sloop forty-six feet at the keel, eighteen feet by the beam, and eight feet in the hold. Harding may have also constructed the periauger *Adventure* in 1725. Periaugers, larger than canoes, often were made from hollowed cypress logs that were widened by splitting the logs to add one or more planks, and were propelled by oars or sail. They were useful for navigating the shallow interior waters of North Carolina. Some, like the *Adventure*, which cleared Bath bound for the York River in Virginia with pitch and a barrel of oil, were sufficiently large to engage in the coastal and West Indies trade. Another craft built in Bath in 1725 was the small, three-ton schooner *Virginity*, which also traded to Virginia.[31]

Modern reproduction of a periauger, designed and constructed at the North Carolina Maritime Museum at Beaufort, and a visitor to Bath during its maiden voyage in 2004.

Over the ensuing half century, shipbuilders in Bath continued to construct as well as repair vessels. A visitor to the town in the mid-1760s remarked that there was "lit[t]le or no trade" but "several vessels" were built in Bath. Indeed, the impressive seventy-ton brig, *Charming Polly*, emerged from the ways in Bath in 1770, though it may have been finished elsewhere because the ship was registered at Port Beaufort. Nevertheless, Bath possessed marine repair capabilities that were lacking in the town of Beaufort. In 1774 the brig *Elizabeth* sailed from Beaufort to Bath, "where the . . . Ship was hove down and underwent a thorough repair—which for want of skilfull and experienced Shipwrights at Beaufort could not be done or performed there."[32]

Large ships or small, Port Bath was an active shipping district at the outset. However, the transfer of the Neuse watershed to the Port Beaufort district in 1730 and the settlement of the Cape Fear with the consequent establishment of Port Brunswick diminished the relative importance of Bath. Port Bath soon lagged behind all of the other shipping districts except the isolated Port Currituck. In 1739 and 1740, 24 and 28 vessels, respectively, entered Port Bath, compared to 41 and 36 for Port Roanoke, 38 and 46 for Port Brunswick, 30 and 40 for Port Roanoke, and 0 and 3 for Port Currituck. According to Gov. Arthur Dobbs, an annual average of 28 ships entered Port Bath from 1748 through 1754, a fact not lost on the General Assembly, which noted in 1759 that "the Trade of Port Bath hath of late . . . [greatly] decreased." Port Bath's position had not changed in 1763, when Dobbs observed that "for many" years past the average number of ships entering Ports Roanoke, Brunswick, Beaufort, Bath, and Currituck was 97, 90, 73, 30, and 6, respectively.[33]

Assuming the validity of those estimates, shipping in North Carolina prior to the Revolution increased appreciably, as shown in Tables 7 and 8, although Port Bath continued to rank fourth among the five customs districts. Port Roanoke witnessed the most activity, averaging 154 entrances and 163 clearances per year from 1768 through 1772, followed by Ports Beaufort (130, 133), Brunswick (128, 125), Bath (51, 55), and Currituck (49, 44). But in terms of volume Port Brunswick easily surpassed the others, importing and exporting an annual average of 9,060 and 8,759 tons, respectively, or 1.3 times the combined total of its nearest rival, Port Roanoke, and 4.3 times the combined import and export tonnage of Port Bath.

Table 7

Number and Tonnage of Ships Entering North Carolina Customs Districts, 1768-1772

	Currituck		Roanoke		Bath		Beaufort		Brunswick	
Year	Number	Tonnage	Number	Tonnage	Number	Tonnage	Number	Tonnage	Number	Tonnage
1768	46	927	153	7,304	40	1,818	128	4,142	105	7,338
1769	51	902	155	6,318	39	1,534	118	4,793	127	9,629
1770	43	846	137	6,097	41	1,586	129	3,812	123	8,622
1771	57	1,385	154	6,559	63	2,507	132	4,405	139	9,935
1772	49	993	169	6,858	70	2,488	144	4,530	147	9,775
Average	49		154		51		130		128	

SOURCE: *See* Table 3.

Table 8

Number and Tonnage of Ships Clearing North Carolina Customs Districts, 1768-1772

	Currituck		Roanoke		Bath		Beaufort		Brunswick	
Year	Number	Tonnage	Number	Tonnage	Number	Tonnage	Number	Tonnage	Number	Tonnage
1768	36	717	161	7,692	50	2,158	120	3,760	118	8,608
1769	55	1,044	172	7,404	42	1,609	133	4,927	117	8,129
1770	48	807	145	6,251	44	1,908	130	4,066	118	8,368
1771	47	1,140	168	6,906	67	2,612	134	4,363	131	9,928
1772	35	604	171	6,807	72	2,423	146	4,508	142	8,763
Average	44		163		55		133		125	

SOURCE: *See* Table 3.

Commercial Enterprises in Bath

Residents or lot owners of Bath reflected the overwhelmingly commercial orientation of the town. Mariners and merchants abounded. Of the former, some were speculators who never lived in the town. John Trimble of Dublin, master of the "Ship called the mary and betsey lying at anchor at the port of Bath," bought a waterfront lot and house in 1730. Samuel Parsons of New Hampshire, "master of the schooner Success, riding anchor at port Bath" in 1740, left a power of attorney with a local resident.[34] Others, like Matthew Rowan, remained in Bath temporarily, eventually finding more lucrative opportunities elsewhere. Still others became permanent citizens. Town commissioner and public official Roger Kenyon, former quartermaster of a privateer, prospered soon after his arrival in Bath about 1720. William Vaughn, "at present in North Carolina" in 1729, bought three lots in town; seven years later he purchased a plantation in Beaufort County.[35] William Rigby settled in Bath in 1738 as did Nathaniel Blin in 1770, both probably encouraged by relatives who lived in the town.[36] Michael Coutanche, "mariner of Boston," brought either money, business acumen, or both to Bath, given the success that he enjoyed at mid-century as a merchant-shipper.[37]

Coutanche represented the ever present and numerous merchant segment of Bath's population. As a port and seat of a shipping district, Bath beckoned to the mercantile class. At any given time, several merchants lived in the town or used it as a base of operations. Resident merchants Edward Porter, John Clarke, and William Jones in 1717 reflected the complexion of Bath's economy throughout the colonial era. During the early 1730s Oliver Blackburn (Blackbourn), Henry Crofton, Edward Broughton, Daniel Blinn, and Robert Cutler, no doubt among others, pursued the mercantile trade. From the time that John Lawson claimed Bonner's Point (originally called Town Point), which jutted out into the water at the junction of Bath and Back Creeks, the favorable location of that property rendered it a particularly busy center of activity. A brick storehouse on lot 7 proved so useful that it was bought and sold independently of the lot. A succession of merchants owned Bonner's Point, including James Calef, agent for James Bowdoin of Boston, John Watson and Alexander Cairnes of Suffolk, Virginia, William Mace, and William Brown.[38]

Some merchants and mariners owned ships, though in the colonial era and later North Carolinians mostly depended upon foreign shipping, mainly from New England and Great Britain, to support their commerce. About ten years after he settled in Bath, Coutanche bought a half interest in the sloop *New Bern*, and soon sent the vessel to Liverpool. James Calef had the misfortune to lose his sloop to a privateer in 1748. In the 1760s William Palmer, son of Robert, and Robert Naval owned the schooner *Dispatch*. Palmer solely owned the *Friendship* and the schooner *Tryon*. Simon Alderson, "Mariner," who briefly possessed the Bonner's Point property in 1768, also owned and sailed the schooner *Sally* to Kingston, Jamaica, in the same year with a cargo of shingles, staves, and lumber.[39]

An artisan population supplemented the mariners and merchants. Thomas Harding, shipwright and town commissioner after 1715, and Michael McDonagh, shipwright, doubtlessly were responsible for most of the early ships built in Bath. Carpenters Robert Potter, William Scott, Thomas Larke (Lark), and Samuel Thomson; bricklayers Thomas Roper and Andrew Connor; and nailer Richard Rigby represented the building trades. Richard Jones, cooper, fashioned barrels necessary for the storage and shipment of naval stores, tobacco, rice, and foodstuffs. Thomas Williams provided blacksmithing services that were so essential to early American life.[40]

Service and professional personnel undergirded the commercial and artisan population. Butcher John Brown prepared the wide variety of meats, including pork, beef, and venison, enjoyed by the colonials. Robert Cutler, saddler, engaged in leatherwork. Tailors William Mitchell, Thomas Owen, and Thomas Armstrong and cordwainer (shoemaker) Daniel Peco made and mended wearing apparel and shoes. Among the professionals were several physicians who temporarily resided in Bath, including Edward Traverse, Wally Chauncy, and Bryan McMahon, and lawyer Wyriot Ormond Sr., town assemblyman. No doubt the services of John Colleson, scrivener, were much in demand.[41]

Arguably the most numerous and active of Bath's business people were tavern keepers. The tavern, more frequently called an ordinary in colonial North Carolina, but also termed a public house (of entertainment), victualing house, and tippling house, constituted one of the bulwarks of provincial institutional life. The tavern not only offered respite to the traveler and comfort to those in its immediate environs, but it also furnished a medium for the conduct of such public affairs as auctions and slave sales, served as a repository for the public mails, and provided a center for political deliberations and machinations. In North Carolina the tavern aroused ambivalent emotions among its patrons, particularly travelers who perhaps were more accustomed to the inns of the northern provinces or to the amenities of European establishments. A few miles north of Bath, William Logan complained of staying in a house with "many air holes," an "Earthen Floor," and a "stinking . . . Bed," but when he arrived in town he admitted that Edward Howcott kept "a very good publick House."[42]

Urban areas such as Bath offered obvious advantages to keepers of public houses. Not only was there a cluster of residents to supply a steady clientele, but Bath also hosted many visitors. As a result Bath usually supported several taverns. Thomas Unday and James Robbins offered competition for Roger Kenyon in the mid-1720s. James Brickell and John Chilly vied for patronage in the late 1730s. Abraham Duncan hosted a meeting of the governor's council in 1744 in his tavern in or near Bath, and probably provided lodging and meals for those distinguished gentlemen. Two years later, detained by inclement weather in December 1746, Gov. Gabriel Johnston spent a week and a half in Duncan's tavern. At the same time Edward Howcott provided services for such travelers as Logan. At least three taverns, run by Mourning Blinn, William Stubbs, and Samuel Taylor, awaited patrons in 1756; and at least two, operated by Mary Smith and Giles Clements, in 1761.[43]

Women played no small role as tavern keepers. According to extant records, they owned almost one-fifth of the public houses in Chowan and Pasquotank Counties, and approximately one-tenth of the ordinaries in Perquimans County before the Revolution. Often maintaining a tavern was an economic necessity, for most of the women were widows who continued their deceased husbands' tavern business. Following the death of her husband, Mourning Blinn kept a tavern in Bath from 1756 through 1758. Mary Smith ran a tavern in the town in 1761, and a Mrs. Bond managed a tavern at Core Point for many years. While most women kept their public houses from one to three years, either remarrying or becoming disillusioned with the arduous task of providing service to the public, some ladies made tavern keeping a permanent occupation.[44]

Taverns doubtlessly represented the best example in early America of a government-regulated business. By law precinct (later county) courts licensed public houses and annually established rates that tavern keepers might legally charge for food, drink, lodging, and the care of animals. The Beaufort County Court in 1761 approved the following rates:

Lodging per night, whole bed	£0.0.8
Hot dinner	0.1.4
Cold dinner	0.0.8
Hot supper	0.1.0
Cold supper	0.0.8
Breakfast	0.0.8
Madeira wine, qt.	0.6.0
Vidonia wine, qt.	0.5.0
Claret qt.	0.5.0
Port or other red wine, qt.	0.5.0

Punch per qt. with loaf sugar and W. I. rum	0.1.8
Punch, qt., with brown sugar	0.1.0
Toddy, qt.	0.1.4
Cider, country, brandy, half pint	0.0.6
Peach, country brandy, half pint	0.0.8
English beer, qt.	0.2.0
N.Y. or Philadelphia beer, qt.	0.2.0
Cider, qt.	0.0.6
N.E. rum, half pint	0.0.8
W.I. rum, half pint	0.1.0
Pasturage each horse 24 hours	0.0.4
Stabling with sufficient fodder or hay per night, each horse, mare, or gilding	0.0.8
Indian corn, qt.	0.0.2[45]

In addition to setting the prices of food, drink, lodging, and stabling and pasturage, the General Assembly imposed other restrictions upon tavern keepers. Legislation forbade "unlawful gaming" in ordinaries, banning in 1764 all games of chance except backgammon. Nine years later the legislature relaxed the prohibition to permit patrons to play whist, quadrille, piquet, and billiards in addition to backgammon. Tavern keepers were also forbidden to allow patrons to become intoxicated or to "drink more than . . . [was] necessary" on the Sabbath, and were not allowed to serve sailors without the permission of their captains, a significant proscription in the case of Bath.[46]

Although tavern keepers played a vital role in Bath's business community, their livelihood, like that of customs collectors, shipbuilders, and butchers, depended mainly upon the commercial traffic generated by the port. The future of Bath looked auspicious early in the eighteenth century when the town became the seat of the customs district. Ships entered Bath from ports throughout the Western world and left for similarly diverse destinations. Captains and their crews wandered the streets and frequented the taverns of Bath, sometimes remaining for a short duration or occasionally settling permanently in the town. Although Bath remained small, its maritime activity increased after the mid-eighteenth century, rendering it a port of some consequence to the Revolution.

NOTES

1. David Stick, *The Outer Banks in North Carolina* (Chapel Hill: University of North Carolina Press, 1958), 8-9; Byron Eugene Logan, "An Historical Geographic Survey of North Carolina Ports" (Ph.D. diss., University of North Carolina, 1956), 13-15, 36-37.

2. Gary S. Dunbar, *Historical Geography of the North Carolina Outer Banks* (Baton Rouge: Louisiana State University Press, 1958), 21, 26, 129-130; Stick, *Outer Banks*, 274-277; Saunders, *Colonial Records*, 3:210; 4:170.

3. Saunders, *Colonial Records*, 4:170; Dunbar, *Historical Geography*, 21, 130; Stick, *Outer Banks*, 303-304; Charles Christopher Crittenden, *The Commerce of North Carolina, 1763-1789* (New Haven: Yale University Press, 1936), 4-5; Richard Lawrence, telephone conversation with author, November 16, 2001.

4. Thomas C. Barrow, *Trade and Empire in Colonial America: The British Customs Service, 1660-1775* (Cambridge, Mass.: Harvard University Press, 1967), 72, 261-264.

5. Saunders, *Colonial Records*, 2:vi, 236-239; Cain, *North Carolina Higher-Court Minutes, 1724-1730*, xxv; Harry Roy Merrens, *Colonial North Carolina in the Eighteenth Century: A Study in Historical Geography* (Chapel Hill: University of North Carolina Press, 1964), 87; Alan D. Watson, "Port Brunswick in the Colonial Era," Lower Cape Fear Historical Society *Journal* 31 (June 1989): 24.

6. Barrow, *Trade and Empire*, 73-78, 261-264.

7. Barrow, *Trade and Empire*, 78; Crittenden, *Commerce in North Carolina*, 39-40; Wilson Angley, "Port Bath, North Carolina, in the Eighteenth Century: A Compilation of Records" (report, Research Branch, Division of Archives and History, Raleigh, 1981), 42.

8. "An Account of Duties Collected and the Fines and Forfeitures recovered in the several ports now under the American Commission, Oct. 10, 1766 and Oct. 10, 1767," Treasury Papers, 1/452, f. 47, photostatic copy, Library of Congress, Washington, D. C. The figure in the report for the deficit for Port Bath was £61.11.2½, owing to a miscalculation of one penny.

9. Clark, *State Records*, 25:194-196; "An Act for facilitating the Navigation of the several Ports of this Province [1738/39]," www.ah.dcr.state.nc.us/sections/hp/colonial/editions/Acts/ports.htm. Powder money, obtained from a duty apparently first imposed in 1715, was initially used for defense, then for navigation improvements. Clark, *State Records*, 23:45-46; Crittenden, *Commerce of North Carolina*, 47, 47 n. 20.

10. Clark, *State Records*, 23:375-378, 438, 475, 506-507, 588-589, 622, 667-672, 745-746, 826-827.

11. Clark, *State Records*, 23:55-56, 639-649, 790-801; 25:313-319, 378-387, for non-tobacco products; 23:402-417, 477-478, 548, 728-741; 25:365-367, 495-496, for tobacco.

12. Clark, *State Records*, 23:212-213, 411; Book 2, p. 449 (microfilm), Beaufort County Deeds; Beaufort County Court Minutes, June term 1758. The Crown's collector of customs in the respective shipping districts often served as receiver of the powder and lead or tonnage duty and the tariff on spirituous liquors. However, in 1755 Gov. Arthur Dobbs appointed Wyriot Ormond rather than collector Robert Palmer receiver of the tonnage duty for Port Bath. Saunders, *Colonial Records*, 5:329.

13. Merrens, *Colonial North Carolina*, 134-140; Janet Schaw, *Journal of a Lady of Quality*, ed. Evangeline Walker Andrews and Charles McLean Andrews (New Haven: Yale University Press, 1923), 166; Alan D. Watson, "Society and Economy in Colonial Edgecombe County," *North Carolina Historical Review* 50 (summer 1973): 249.

14. Merrens, *Colonial North Carolina*, 120-131; Angley, "Port Bath," 22.

15. Lawson, *New Voyage to Carolina*, 104; Merrens, *Colonial North Carolina*, 97-106.

16. Lawson, *New Voyage to Carolina*, 104; "Journal of a French Traveller in the Colonies, I," *American Historical Review* 26 (July 1921): 733; John Ferdinand Dalziel Smyth, *A Tour in the United States of America*, 2 vols. (1784; reprint, New York: Arno Press, 1968), 2:95-96; Crittenden, *Commerce in North Carolina*, 53-54. For the distinction between tar and green tar, see Crittenden, *Commerce in North Carolina*, 56, and Lee, *Lower Cape Fear in Colonial Days*, 153-154.

17. Saunders, *Colonial Records*, 2:237; "Journal of a French Traveller," 733-734; Smyth, *Tour*, 2:96-97; Crittenden, *Commerce in North Carolina*, 54-56; Merrens, *Colonial North Carolina*, 85-87, 89.

18. Merrens, *Colonial North Carolina*, 90-91; Angley, "Port Bath," 10-32.

19. Merrens, *Colonial North Carolina*, 93-97; Angley, "Port Bath," 24.

20. Angley, "Port Bath," 18, 22, 24, 26.

21. Angley, "Port Bath," 19, 20, 21, 23.

22. Ledger of Imports and Exports, British North American Ports, 1768-1773, Customs, 16/1, British Public Record Office, Photocopies, Southern Historical Collection, Chapel Hill, N.C.

23. Angley, "Port Bath," 19, 21, 22.

24. Angley, "Port Bath," 92.

25. Crittenden, *Commerce in North Carolina*, 79-83; Angley, "Port Bath," 14, 15, 25, 26.

26. Clark, *State Records*, 23:45-46, 268-272, 308-309, 371-375, 395-398, 680; 25:361-364; An Act for laying a Duty on Liquors for and towards defraying the contingent Charges of the Government [1734/35], www.ah.dcr.state.nc.us/sections/hp/colonial/editions/Acts/duty.htm; Saunders, *Colonial Records*, 7:434; Angley, "Port Bath," 52-57.

27. Customs 16/1.

28. Crittenden, *Commerce in North Carolina*, 9-11; Joseph Goldenberg, "Names and Numbers: Statistical Notes on Some Port Records of Colonial North Carolina," *American Neptune* 29 (1969): 155-157. For Port Brunswick, which featured larger vessels, see Watson, "Port Brunswick," 26-27.

29. Angley, "Port Bath," 11, 52-57.

30. Customs 16/1.

31. Book 1, pp. 239-240 (microfilm), Beaufort County Deeds; "The Tool Bag," *Tributaries* 2 (1992): 31-33; Angley, "Port Bath," 10. Harding's shipyard was among the first in North Carolina.

32. "Journal of a French Traveller," 736; Angley, "Port Bath," 28-29.

33. Saunders, *Colonial Records*, 5:314; 6:968; Clark, *State Records*, 23:507; Angley, "Port Bath," 3-4.

34. Book 2, pp. 28-29, 338 (microfilm), Beaufort County Deeds.

35. Book 1, p. 517; Book 2, p. 248 (microfilm), Beaufort County Deeds.

36. Book 2, pp. 269-270; Book 4, pp. 260-261 (microfilm), Beaufort County Deeds.

37. Book 2, p. 331 (microfilm), Beaufort County Deeds.

38. Book 1, pp. 224, 225, 238-239; Book 2, pp. 94-95, 107-108, 133, 175-176, 193-194; Book 3, pp. 102, 217, 225-226; Book 4, pp. 199, 202-203, 238 (microfilm), Beaufort County Deeds; Angley, "Bonner House Vicinity of Bath," 26-27, 35-37.

39. Book 2, p. 522; Book 3, pp. 69, 87; Book 4, pp. 202-203 (microfilm), Beaufort County Deeds; Angley, "Port Bath," 23-26.

40. Book 1, pp. 239-240, 279-280, 458; Book 2, pp. 27, 89, 168, 269-270, 280-281; Book 3, pp. 74, 385; Book 4, p. 374 (microfilm), Beaufort County Deeds.

41. Book 2, pp. 133, 173, 280-281, 293, 394-395, 500-501; Book 3, p. 445; Book 4, pp. 257-258, 273 (microfilm), Beaufort County Deeds.

42. "William Logan's Journal of a Journey to Georgia, 1745," *Pennsylvania Magazine of History and Biography* 36 (1912): 10; Alan D. Watson, "The Colonial Tavern: A Gathering Place in the Albemarle," in *A Taste of the Past: Foodways of the Albemarle Region, 1585-1830*, ed. Barbara E. Taylor (Elizabeth City, N.C.: The Museum of the Albemarle, 1991), 36.

43. Cain, *North Carolina Higher-Court Minutes, 1724-1730*, 163-164; Book 1, p. 428; Book 2, pp. 260, 263-264, 371-372, 519 (microfilm), Beaufort County Deeds; Saunders, *Colonial Records*, 4:743, 1178; Beaufort County Court Minutes, June term 1756, September term 1757, June term 1761. The legislature in 1715 exempted residents and freeholders of Bath for ten years from paying a license fee to retail liquors in the town if the beverages were manufactured in Bath County. Clark, *State Records*, 23:75.

44. Beaufort County Court Minutes, June term 1756, September term 1757, June term 1761; Hugh Buckner Johnston, ed., "The Journal of Ebenezer Hazard in North Carolina, 1777 and 1778," *North Carolina Historical Review* 36 (July 1959): 371; Watson, "Colonial Tavern," 37.

45. Beaufort County Court Minutes, June term 1761.

46. Clark, *State Records*, 23:183-185, 492-494, 611, 725-728; 25:262, 358.

4

Society

Bath as a Small Town in Eastern North Carolina

Although Bath was the first incorporated town in North Carolina, it remained relatively small, quite overshadowed by Edenton and New Bern, its immediate neighbors to the north and south, respectively. Water constituted the key to trade in the colonial era. Edenton took advantage of the traffic on the Chowan River and Albemarle Sound, and New Bern pulled from a large hinterland served by the Neuse and Trent Rivers. Bath, though sited close to the Pamlico River, found the river and Bath and Back Creeks less promising for commercial purposes. Moreover, given the ravages of the Tuscarora War in Bath County, Edenton upon its founding was quickly favored over Bath as the "metropolis" of the colony. Afterwards, as settlement proceeded southward along the coast and eventually encompassed the Cape Fear region, New Bern became the most centrally located town in eastern North Carolina, and thus the logical site for a permanent capital. The General Assembly in 1746 briefly accorded Bath consideration as the provincial capital, but the eventual decision to favor New Bern virtually dashed all hopes for Bath to become an urban community of significant size.[1]

Initially Bath struggled to overcome the effects of the Tuscarora War, but recovery was slow. In 1714 the town boasted perhaps no more than nine houses. A decade and a half later, however, naturalist John Brickell referred to Bath as the "Second considerable Town" (following Edenton) in the province. As Quaker traveler William Logan passed through the town in 1745, he counted approximately thirty houses, representing perhaps the peak of Bath's population, for in 1754 Gov. Arthur Dobbs reported that Bath contained only about twenty families,

Life-styles of Early Bath County Residents: Inventories and Wills

When a person of means died during the colonial period, one or more documents may have recorded the estate of the deceased. Probate law required the compilation of an inventory of the assets not disposed of by last will and testament. Executors and administrators usually listed and appraised only the moveable property that might be hidden from creditors or stolen; real estate was rarely included in an inventory. Since inventories list the entire undisposed contents of households, down to the last cracked and battered earthenware pot, they provide excellent sources for the study of the material conditions of Bath's early residents. To a lesser degree, the same holds true for wills, which often contain specific legacies to family members and friends.

The few surviving Bath County inventories from the turn of the eighteenth century show that material possessions for most residents on this frontier were meager. The items listed reflect primarily the concerns of daily survival—tools necessary for clearing forests, raising crops, and constructing buildings, livestock for farming and food, canoes for travel, and guns for protection and hunting. Most homes were small, one-room structures where the business of food preparation, eating, sleeping, living, and dying all took place. Most households had but little furniture; the most commonly enumerated pieces were beds and chests. Tables and chairs did not begin to appear regularly in household inventories until later in the century. Most families ate from earthenware bowls and wooden trenchers held in their laps as they perched on crates and chests or sat on the floor. Amenities were few and even many of the basic necessities inventoried were described as "old" or in disrepair. Among the goods of James Hogg, whose estate was appraised in 1707, were "2 old guns without locks" and "2 old linen wheels."

Representative of the lower ranks of Bath society was Uriah Cannon, who appears to have eked out a spartan existence at the turn of the century. His 1702 inventory revealed that he and his family members slept on two bed

compared to fifty in Edenton and ninety in Wilmington. At the outset of the Revolution, United States postal inspector Ebenezer Hazard also found only twenty houses in Bath.[2] While Edenton, New Bern, and Wilmington thrived along the coast, Bath, along with Beaufort and Brunswick Town, stagnated, surviving principally because they were seats of their respective customs districts.

ticks (probably stuffed with corn husks) placed directly on the floor. No bed linen was listed; blankets and a rug served as bed clothing. During the day, this bedding would have been rolled up and stored out of the way. The only piece of furniture recorded in the inventory was a chest, which probably served multiple functions in the Cannon household. In addition to storing the family's clothing and other items, it could have also been used as a table for preparing and serving meals and even as a place to sit. An earthen pot, a tin saucepan, and three bowls constituted the household's scant assemblage of kitchenware. A tub and pail were probably called into duty for washing clothes and dishes, cleaning vegetables, and processing meat. Three hogs, a heifer, and a calf made up the sum total of the livestock. Meat likely appeared infrequently on the Cannon family menu and most often in small quantities as a seasoning for vegetables and grain-based dishes.

The Cannon household was representative of that of many of the area's settlers, who were poor families working small farms. The opposite end of the economic spectrum was illustrated in another inventory prepared in 1702, that of some of the household goods owned by Thomas Dearham. Dearham first acquired property in Bath County in 1701, obtaining large tracts of land through the headright system. The display of material wealth in his home—a mirrored looking glass and two wooden bedsteads topped with feather mattresses, pillows, and bolsters encased in linens—evidences a more extravagant life-style. An array of pewter plates, dishes, tankards and porringers, a glistening copper stew pan, a brass skillet, and several large brass kettles bespoke his culinary refinement and ability to entertain guests. With sixty hogs and fourteen cows, Dearham's family would not have needed to restrict their diet to the starchy stews and porridges common to the lower and middling ranks of society. Twelve guns, plus pistols, two rapiers, and a curved scimitar made an impressive display of weaponry for hunting and self-defense. Such extravagant living apparently came at a price for Dearham, however. Unlike Cannon, Dearham's inventory was prepared while he was still alive, in compliance with legal action taken to settle his debts.

Getting to Bath in the Colonial Era

Aiding Bath's survival was its location along the lone highway through North Carolina, sometimes called the King's Highway, which led from Virginia to South Carolina. The road ran from Suffolk, Virginia, to Edenton, Bath, New Bern, Wilmington, Brunswick Town, and Georgetown, South Carolina. At a time when overland travel was arduous and communication was restricted, the highway together with the nearby Pamlico River offered Bath exposure to the outside world.

Approximately forty miles separated Bath from Albemarle Sound to the north, where a ferry crossed to Edenton. The journey often took two days for travelers, though the Reverend George Whitefield started at daybreak on December 22, 1739, and arrived at Bath at eight o'clock in the evening. After crossing the Pamlico River, another thirty-five to forty miles had to be covered to reach New Bern to the south, and that required a full day of hard travel, including the ferriage across the Neuse River. Again, the indefatigable Whitefield covered the distance in a single day.[3]

The rigors of overland travel were daunting in early North Carolina. The road from Albemarle Sound through Tyrrell County to Bath crossed some of the most melancholy, desolate terrain in North Carolina, called the Great Alligator Dismal Swamp. Whitefield commented on the wet, swampy ground and the uninhabited country. Ebenezer Hazard agreed, writing that the area was "very poor, & mostly low, sunken Land." Elkanah Watson found the "dreariness . . . scarcely relieved by the appearance of a house, except a few miserable tar burners' huts." The road from Bath (after crossing the Pamlico River) to New Bern improved. Hazard remarked about the posts that were fixed by the roadside on which the number of miles was marked in roman numerals and notches, the latter, he supposed, for the benefit of the unlearned. Relief was occasionally realized by a "sweet breeze," the "serenade of innumerable songsters of the forest," or the "Great troops or flocks of swine" that ran wild in the woods. Between Bath and New Bern, Watson chased a wild turkey "who maintained his equal right to the road, like a true North Carolina republican," and eventually outdistanced his pursuers.[4]

Where fords and bridges were inadequate to cross the watercourses that interdicted the roads, the colonials resorted to ferries. Precinct or county courts determined the location of the ferry, the types of boats needed for transport, and the rates that might be charged for passage. Recipients of ferry licenses were required to post a bond as a guarantee for maintaining proper boats and attendance at the ferries. Regardless of the legal strictures, ferriage in North Carolina often proved unreliable, if not dangerous. Adverse winds and rough waters occasioned delays as did the failure of the ferry keepers to provide service. According to Johann Schoepf, "Travellers [in North Carolina] therefore must have a good supply of patience if they are not to be outdone at extreme carelessness [at the ferries] which may often mean hindrance and loss to them." Moreover, ferry boats were deemed "none of the best," "not very good," and "very bad." Together with poor roads and bridges, ferriage at best slowed travel perceptibly.[5]

Approaching Bath from the north or south necessitated contending with the most formidable ferry crossings in North Carolina. To the north the road from Virginia required crossing the Albemarle Sound, a lengthy passage that was likened by one traveler to crossing the English Channel. From the south, the road leading from New Bern to Bath presented a ferry crossing at the Neuse River before

Sketch of a colonial ferry transporting a horse and carriage.

reaching the Pamlico River, where another ferry linked Core Point on the south bank to Bath on the north. Estimated at three to five miles by travelers, the Core Point ferriage run took William Logan two and a half hours. Although the Beaufort County Court had early established a public ferry from Bath to Core Point, by 1740 it had ceased to operate, largely because private individuals were carrying people across the Pamlico there at reduced rates. Thus in 1740 the General Assembly instructed the court to appoint another ferry keeper from Bath to Core Point, and prohibited anyone from ferrying passengers over the river within ten miles of the public ferry. In return, the ferry keeper was expected to construct a road south from Core Point, erect a tavern "fit to entertain Travellers," and provide appropriate boats and canoes to transport passengers and their horses.[6]

A succession of men and women kept the Bath-Core Point ferry. The Beaufort County Court in 1756 entrusted the ferry to Grizle Hardy, widow. Three years later John Freeman replaced Mrs. Hardy. By 1765 a Mrs. Bond, probably the widow of John Bond, operated the ferry, which she retained as late as 1778. The county courts frequently licensed widows of ferry keepers to continue their deceased husbands' business, for otherwise the women lacked a ready means of support. Of course, servants, slaves, or male members of the family provided the labor. Bond's ferry offered "open" boats, probably canoes, which Hugh Finlay characterized as "not very good."[7]

Blackbeard and Bath

Upon entering Bath travelers encountered an array of town folks, ranging from mariners, merchants, and artisans to professionals, government officials, and even alleged pirates, specifically Blackbeard, one of the most feared of the "brethren of the black flag." When Blackbeard trod the streets of Bath, he briefly left behind the dangers and privations of life at sea in the eighteenth century. Still, the lure of adventure and the anticipation of sharing the loot from a captured prize tempered the hardships.[8]

Actually, so little is known about Blackbeard that most of his life remains shrouded in legend and lore. Scholars have been unable to even determine his true name. Contemporaries referred to him as Thatch (Tach, Thach, Tatch); later writers, as Edward Teach. He may have been born in Bristol, England, but possibly in London, Philadelphia, or elsewhere. Although usually depicted as a large, frightful, savage figure, according to one of his captors, he "was a tall Spare Man with a very black beard which he wore very long." Blackbeard burst on the historical scene in 1717, probably after a stint of privateering in Queen Anne's War and a subsequent apprenticeship in piracy under the notorious Benjamin Hornigold. Blackbeard quickly became the scourge of the Atlantic, cultivating a reputation for wanton cruelty. He collected a flotilla of ships, including a vessel that belonged to Major Stede Bonnet, the "gentleman pirate" from Barbados, whose inexperience rendered him distinctly subordinate to Blackbeard. Prowling the Atlantic and Caribbean for several months in 1717 and 1718, Blackbeard took numerous prizes, including the French slaver *Concorde*, which he renamed *Queen Anne's Revenge*. After blockading Charleston, South Carolina, in May 1718, taking several ships and embarrassing the government, Blackbeard made his way up the coast to Beaufort (formerly Old Topsail) Inlet, where the *Queen Anne's Revenge* grounded and sank.[9]

Blackbeard then sailed a small Spanish sloop that he had captured to Bath, where he and twenty crewmen accepted pardons under the Act of Grace from Gov. Charles Eden. The governor convened a court of vice-admiralty that condemned the Spanish sloop as a prize and granted full ownership of it to Blackbeard. During the ensuing few weeks the former pirate reputedly resided in Bath, where he lived lavishly and supposedly married the teenage daughter of a nearby planter. After a few weeks Blackbeard took his sloop to sea, where he looted several English ships and captured two French vessels, one of which he brought back to Bath, where he told the governor that he had found it drifting at sea. Another court of vice-admiralty declared the vessel a derelict, allowing Blackbeard to claim salvage rights. Some of its cargo eventually found its way under questionable circumstances into the possession of Governor Eden and Chief Justice Tobias Knight, who lived in the vicinity of Bath. Fearing perhaps that the ship might be recognized, Blackbeard told the governor that the vessel was unseaworthy, whereupon Eden granted him permission to burn and sink it.[10]

Blackbeard tarried along the North Carolina coast, occasionally perhaps in Bath, for several months, often, it seems, engaging in petty theft with impunity. Finding Governor Eden unwilling or unable to protect the citizenry, some North Carolinians, including Maurice Moore and Edward Moseley, appealed to Virginia governor Alexander Spotswood for aid. Although he had done little for North Carolina during the Tuscarora War, Spotswood dispatched two ships, manned by marines of the Royal Navy and volunteer

Edward Teach, or Thatch, known to history as Blackbeard, was probably an occasional resident of Bath.

sailors. They found Blackbeard at Ocracoke Inlet in November 1718. In a fierce, bloody struggle, the Virginians, led by Lt. Robert Maynard of the Royal Navy, killed Blackbeard and captured or killed his crew. The hand-to-hand combat, featuring pistols, cutlasses, and axes, lasted but a few minutes. Blackbeard sought out Maynard. Both men fired at one another and Blackbeard was hit in the chest, but the ball failed to stop him. As he lunged toward Maynard with his cutlasses, Blackbeard was staggered by a blow from behind. Weakened by multiple cuts and gunshot wounds, the pirate leader fell to the deck. When the battle concluded, Maynard severed Blackbeard's head and hung it from the bowsprit of his sloop as he sailed triumphantly back to Virginia.

Among Blackbeard's possessions was a letter and account book that seemingly incriminated Tobias Knight, indicating that he had received stolen property from Blackbeard. But Knight later successfully defended himself in court against charges of accessory to piracy. Governor Eden, about whom swirled rumors of conspiracy with Blackbeard, was never implicated in any illegal activity. In fact, after taking the Act of Grace in June 1718, Blackbeard technically committed no acts of piracy and was killed during an unauthorized invasion of North Carolina from Virginia. In any event, more than 275 years later, Blackbeard thrust himself pressingly on historical consciousness and public imagination with the discovery in 1996 of a wreck in Beaufort Inlet that most probably was his flagship, *Queen Anne's Revenge*.[11]

Gov. Charles Eden, intimately involved in the Blackbeard affair, briefly resided in Bath or its immediate environs. Born in England in 1673, Eden received his gubernatorial appointment in 1713, and arrived in North Carolina the following year to assume control of the colony as the Tuscarora War concluded. He moved to Bath in 1716. Eden owned ten lots in Bath but lived on a four-hundred-acre plantation, Thistleworth, on the west bank of Bath Creek near its mouth. He later sold that property, and in 1719 relocated to present-day Bertie County where he lived at Eden House, his plantation, until his death in 1722. Although Eden was most solicitous of the welfare of the Anglican Church, the ever caustic missionary John Urmstone described the governor as "a complete ruffian, . . . a boatswain's mate, . . . fit only to command the forecastle Gang." Continued Urmstone, "Seeing the Genius and temper of the People [of North Carolina] are so like the . . . Gentry, there cannot be a fitter man [than Eden] to govern them." Governor Eden, however, preferred to be remembered by his epitaph: "[he] governed the province eight years to ye greatest satisfaction of ye Lords Proprietors and ye ease and happyness of ye people. He brought ye country into a flourishing Condition and died much lamented."[12]

Other than the governor, Bath's most eminent early citizen was Christopher Gale. Born in York, England, about 1679, the son of the Reverend Miles Gale and Margaret Stone, Gale immigrated to North Carolina at the end of the seventeenth century, settling in Perquimans Precinct. About 1700 Gale moved to Bath County, where he engaged in the Indian trade and shipping. Self-advancement and an imperious character often placed him at odds with the governors of North Carolina. Still, Gale received a commission in 1703 as a member of the General Court, the supreme court of the province, and in 1712 was named chief justice of the court, a position that he apparently occupied until 1731, four years before his death. During the course of his career, Gale served as an emissary to South Carolina during the Tuscarora War to seek aid for North Carolina, held a commission as colonel of the Bath County militia, obtained appointments as collector of customs successively at Ports Beaufort, Currituck, and Roanoke, and represented the colony in a party that surveyed the boundary between North Carolina and Virginia in 1728. Gale spent much of his early years in North Carolina in Bath. He purchased lots in the town in 1706, owned a part interest in a gristmill in Bath, and was a worthy patron of the Church of England in the community.[13]

Among other occupants of Bath was Roger Kenyon, formerly quartermaster of the privateer *Movil (Moville) Trader*, who resided in the town as early as 1720, and quickly achieved prominence, indicative of the upward mobility that was possible in a newly settled society. Buying four waterfront lots, Kenyon worked as a merchant and tavern keeper. Eventually he became a town commissioner of Bath. Kenyon served as provost marshal of Bath County in 1722, and as a justice of the peace and captain of the militia of Beaufort Precinct. Subsequently he represented Bath in the General Assembly in 1731 as the town's first delegate, and again in 1734-1735. Although occupying several responsible public positions and considered a "gentleman," Kenyon some-times found himself at odds with his fellow citizens, including Matthew Rowan and George Burrington, both of whom Kenyon accused of assault.[14]

Pastel portrait of Chief Justice Christopher Gale by Henrietta Johnston, ca. 1719.

Matthew Rowan, acting governor of North Carolina from 1753 to 1754, first lived in Bath upon coming to the colony. Born in Ireland of Scottish parents, Rowan appeared in Bath at least as early as 1726 as a merchant, and as a churchwarden of St. Thomas Parish. He allegedly came to North Carolina to build one or more ships for unnamed persons in Dublin and then absconded with one of the vessels, fully loaded. In any case, he prospered, and had relocated to the Lower Cape Fear region by 1734, where he occupied a plantation in New Hanover (present Brunswick) County. On the recommendation of George Burrington, the proprietors named Rowan to the royal council in 1730, a post that he retained until his death in 1760. Following the death of Gov. Gabriel Johnston in 1752, Nathaniel Rice, president of the council, served as acting governor of the colony. Upon Rice's death in 1753, Rowan, as president of the council, assumed the office of acting governor until the arrival of Gov. Arthur Dobbs in 1754.[15]

Michael Coutanche's First Home in Bath?

Michael Coutanche purchased property in Bath in 1739 and is credited with building the impressive Palmer-Marsh House around 1751. At least a decade before that construction, however, a smaller building stood on the same lot. The archaeological traces of the structure provide some of the best clues to date about the appearance of Bath's buildings in the first half of the eighteenth century.

In 1960, an excavation in the north yard of the Palmer-Marsh House uncovered traces of a twenty-seven-by-seventeen-foot structure built in the 1730s. A brick chimney stood at the north end of this frame building, which rested on underpinnings of brick. The building was probably a story or a story and a half tall, and its dimensions suggest a two-room floor plan. Beneath the southern half lay a cellar constructed of stones that had arrived as ballast in the holds of sailing ships that docked at Bath.

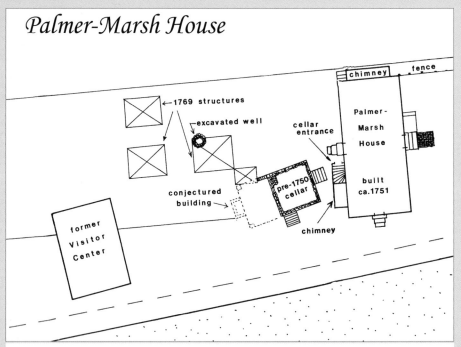

Lot plan of the Palmer-Marsh House and vicinity, showing archaeological vestiges of other historic structures on the property.

Coutanche may have lived in that building in the decade prior to the construction of the Palmer-Marsh House. Pieces of window glass etched with the letters "Michael Cout …" were found during the excavation. Despite its proximity to the new dwelling, the earlier structure remained standing for at least a decade after the completion of the Palmer-Marsh House. Archaeological and documentary evidence indicates subsequent use as one of several stores Coutanche owned on the property. Coutanche traded largely in naval stores, and his ships regularly routed barrels of tar from Bath to Liverpool. Archaeologists found a large quantity of tar on the brick floor of the cellar, possibly spilled from a broken or forgotten barrel intended for the English trade. An entrance into the cellar along the building's north wall allowed easy access to Main Street and the nearby wharves on Bath Creek for loading and unloading naval supplies and other goods.

By the time the Sauthier map of Bath was completed in 1769, the 1730s structure was no longer standing. Brick rubble and wood timbers found on

Excavated cellar of 1730s building behind the Palmer-Marsh House.

the cellar floor suggest that the building was razed and the chimney pushed into the open cellar hole. Household trash, including fragments of a fine black earthenware teapot decorated with gold gilt, a jaw harp, broken wine bottles, turkey and pig bones, and clay tobacco pipes, was tossed in on top of the building debris. A three-foot thick layer of clay, probably from the digging of another cellar somewhere nearby, completed the filling of the cellar. Why the building was destroyed remains a mystery.

About 1740, Michael Coutanche, like Rowan a former mariner, arrived in Bath. Captain Coutanche opened a store and quickly became one of the town's most eminent citizens. He was elected to represent Bath in the General Assembly in 1745, from 1746 to 1752, and from 1758 to 1761. He was appointed a justice of the peace by the governor, and legislation in 1745 designated Coutanche a commissioner of the town of Bath. In addition to his public duties, Coutanche prospered. He purchased seven lots in Bath, six hundred acres adjoining the town, and additional property along the Pamlico River and Pantego Creek. His mercantile business grew so rapidly that by 1758 he needed two stores to vend his merchandise. Attesting to his wealth was the Palmer-Marsh House, a large Georgian structure and the finest house in Bath, which he built in 1751. Following his death in 1761, Coutanche's widow, Sarah, married the Reverend Alexander Stewart.[16]

Stewart, an Irish Anglican minister, immigrated to the colony in 1753. He was subsequently appointed by the Society for the Propagation of the Gospel missionary to St. Thomas Parish, which encompassed Bath and Beaufort County. Born in County Antrim, Ireland, in 1723, and graduated by the University of Dublin, Stewart served Glenary and Loughguile Parishes in County Antrim before going to America. Stewart may have brought a wife and two sons to Bath, all of whom died soon after their arrival. The minister married possibly four more times during his ministry at Bath. One of his wives was Penelope Johnston, daughter of Samuel Johnston and niece of Gov. Gabriel Johnston. It was a union that brought property and an entrée into the political elite of the colony to Stewart. Stewart occupied the glebe house of St. Thomas Parish upon its completion. After two years, he moved to a plantation on Durham's Creek, just east of Bath on the south side of the Pamlico River, where he kept a ferry over the creek. Stewart's health began to fail in the late 1760s, after being injured in the great 1769 hurricane. Suffering from debilitating rheumatism, he succumbed to an unknown illness in the spring of 1771.[17]

Eventually purchasing the Coutanche house was Robert Palmer, Bath's most prominent citizen during the two decades preceding the Revolution. Born in Scotland in 1725, Palmer immigrated to North Carolina in 1753 and settled in Bath. He held royal commissions as surveyor general of North Carolina and collector of customs for the Port of Bath. Together the positions provided Palmer with an annual salary of £1,050, making him perhaps the highest paid royal officer in North Carolina. Palmer also represented Bath in the lower house of the General Assembly in 1762. Upon the recommendation of Gov. Arthur Dobbs, the Crown in 1764 named Palmer to the royal council, which made him a member of the upper house of the legislature. In addition Palmer was colonel of the Beaufort County militia, a member of the commission in 1767 that surveyed the Cherokee boundary in the west, and a lieutenant general of the royal forces during the Regulator campaign in 1768. After Gov. William Tryon appointed Palmer secretary and clerk to the

Crown in 1770, Palmer moved the next year to New Bern, the colonial capital, in order to satisfy the demands of those positions. In 1771, he transferred all of his houses and lots in Bath and fifteen slaves to his son William. His wife Margaret, who died in 1765, is buried in St. Thomas Church.[18]

Given his wealth, social standing, and commodious house, Palmer entertained constantly. According to Elkanah Watson, "Travellers with any pretensions to respectability seldom stop at the wretched taverns, but custom sanctions their freely calling at any planter's residence, who seems to consider himself the party obliged by this freedom." An unnamed Frenchman, passing through Bath in 1765, was invited by Palmer to spend the evening. The visit eventuated in a three-day sojourn with Palmer. Gov. William Tryon was a frequent guest, calling upon Palmer for personal and business reasons. According to the governor, "He had a very excellent house and Plantation at Bath which I often resided in with my family being Hospitably entertained by him." In 1773, Josiah Quincy Jr., a Massachusetts lawyer who went to North Carolina to coordinate colonial opposition to British policies, carried a letter of introduction to Palmer, but found that his prospective host no longer lived in Bath, and, in fact, had left North Carolina for England.[19]

Soon after moving to New Bern, a serious illness beset Palmer, which compelled him to sail to England to regain his health. Continued poor health forced Palmer to remain abroad. He resigned his collectorship in 1772 and seat on the council in 1775, suggesting that his son William succeed him in both positions. In the meantime, William managed his father's properties in North Carolina, remitting from £800 to £1,200 annually to Robert between 1772 and 1776. Palmer was still in England when the war for independence broke out. During the Revolution, the General Assembly declared Robert Palmer a Loyalist and seized his property under the Confiscation Acts of 1777 and 1779. At the request of Palmer, his old friend Richard Caswell in 1785 petitioned the General Assembly to return Palmer's assets, but to no avail. Palmer lodged a claim of £8,103 against the British government for losses suffered because of his loyalty to the Crown. The Loyalist Claims Commission awarded him a payment of £87 and a pension of £300 per annum from 1788 until his death.[20]

Women in Bath

In a male dominated society, women infrequently assumed a public presence. Most who did were single, usually widows. Married women were relegated principally to domestic duties, such as overseeing the household, assuming responsibility for meals and the garden, and caring for children. Single women, however, enjoyed considerable autonomy in business and legal affairs, but of course had to find means to support themselves. Such women headed 5 and 6 percent of the households in Beaufort County in 1755 and 1764, respectively. Most were widows, left in charge of plantations following the deaths of their husbands. Some independent women appeared in Bath, turning to ferry keeping or tavern keeping as a means of livelihood. Jane Caila, however, benefited from the support of her son and a slave. Not so fortunate was Mary Cotton, who in 1724 stole sheets, shirts, and money from Roger Kenyon. Though she pleaded not guilty, a jury convicted her of theft. The court ordered Cotton whipped thirty-one lashes and required her to post bond for her proper behavior in the future.[21]

Only a few women owned lots in Bath. Among them was Isabella Lawson, daughter of John Lawson, who in 1717 purchased her deceased father's property on Town Point, or lots 5 and 6, including the houses and outbuildings. Later that same year Mary Clarke bought lot 29 adjacent to lot 28 that belonged to her father John Clarke. Although Mary Clarke may not have actually lived on her property, at least two women bought lots and built homes. Within three years of acquiring lot 59, Mary Aldershire (Aldershair, Aldershare),

Robert Palmer, the most prominent resident of colonial Bath, suffered financially for his loyalty to the Crown.

"spinster," had built a house, which she sold in 1734 to carpenter Thomas Larke, including all "beds, blankets, sheets, pewter, Brass, Iron, pots, furniture & appurtenances." Six years later, after acquiring lapsed lot 64, Margaret Pendergrass erected the requisite "good substantial habitable house" needed to retain possession of the lot.[22]

African Americans in Bath

African Americans comprised a distinctive element of Bath's population. In the Fundamental Constitutions of Carolina, a plan of government adopted for their colony in 1669, the Lords Proprietors sanctioned the institution of slavery.[23] Most of the slaves who lived in North Carolina in the late seventeenth and early eighteenth centuries were brought overland from Virginia and South Carolina, or by ship from the West Indies.

When African Americans first arrived in the Bath area is unknown, but their appearance likely coincided with the initial European settlement at the end of the seventeenth century. By the turn of the eighteenth century, individuals of African descent were regularly included in the headright lists for land patented around Bath. For example, Joseph Ming listed thirteen black men and women among the twenty-four persons whose transport into the colony he financed in 1701.

Although their presence in surviving documents is sporadic, slaves formed an integral part of the economy of Bath and the surrounding area. The labor of enslaved African Americans was critical to the production of commercial crops, beginning with the initial clearing of fields from the forests—cutting trees, grubbing stumps, and digging drainage ditches—as well as planting and harvesting tobacco, corn, and wheat. The naval stores industry, with its production of tar, pitch, rosin and turpentine, was largely accomplished with slave labor. Slaves also helped produce other forest products crucial to the economy of the area: staves, shingles, and sawn lumber. Early court records indicate that enslaved African Americans toiled alongside white and Native American indentured laborers. In 1701, Dido, a black woman, worked on the plantation of Capt. Nicholas Jones with two white indentured males and a Native American man named Peter. Dido and two of the other three laborers had arrived in the Bath area as headrights of Captain Jones.

Slaves appeared in 32 and 37 percent of Beaufort County families in 1755 and 1764, respectively, and comprised 40 percent of the county taxables (white males sixteen years of age and older, whites married to blacks, and all blacks, twelve years of age and older) in 1755 and 51 percent in 1764. While there were some Bath residents with ten or more slaves (for example, John Maule and Alexander Stewart were taxed in 1764 for eleven and nineteen slaves, respectively), most slave owners in Beaufort County owned only a few bondsmen. Although most lived and toiled on farms and plantations, slaves in port towns like Bath labored along the docks or waterfront as stevedores. Blacks also worked extensively, though not always lawfully, as watermen, bringing small craft from the interior to Bath. In addition, they piloted vessels along the rivers and sounds from Ocracoke Inlet to Bath, Edenton, and New Bern, much to the consternation of white pilots, who complained about the illegal competition offered by blacks. Some slaves, however, worked mainly indoors as household servants for the wealthier whites in Bath. Two years after arriving in town, royal officeholder Robert Palmer claimed four black taxables.[24]

The lives of bondsmen were regulated by a slave code, a body of laws that demanded strict segregation of the races and curtailed the activity of slaves. Of course, slaves easily and often evaded the legal restrictions, and seemed to possess a relative freedom of movement in the larger towns of North Carolina. Nonetheless, slavery remained a harsh institution. Catherine Phillips, an English Quaker missionary who visited Bath in 1754, recounted her experiences during a stay at a tavern in town. An enslaved girl who worked at the tavern fell asleep at the top of the stairs, near Phillips's room. The tavern keeper grew enraged and kicked the girl down the stairs, much to Phillips's disgust and disapproval.[25]

Whites had to guard against evidences of slave dissatisfaction, which ranged from feigning illness, criminal activity, and running away, to insurrection. One particularly interesting case in November 1748 concerned an escape from the Bath jail by Stephen, a slave from Virginia. Stephen, accused of stealing a horse, was assisted in his jailbreak by Jack, an enslaved man belonging to Bath area resident Edward Howcutt. In the dead of night, Jack brought Stephen a long piece of iron, which the jailed man used to break his handcuffs and the lock on the jail door. Stephen escaped through a trap door in the floor of the jail, and Jack carried the shackled man down to the water, where they crossed the creek in a canoe. After hiding out at Howcutt's plantation until the next night, the two men returned to town to secure a file, presumably to break Stephen's leg shackles. Jack proceeded to break into the stores of Mr. Simpson and Mr. Rieusset, in search of a file. He also stole items that could have been used to help Stephen run away—bottles of rum, food, clothing, buttons, knives, and a watch. Jack was apprehended while breaking into the second store but managed to escape by canoe. Stephen was convicted of theft and hanged in mid-December. The fate of his accomplice, Jack, is unknown.[26]

Not coincidentally, perhaps, the onset of the Revolution witnessed the greatest threat of a slave insurrection in North Carolina during the colonial era, when bondsmen in the eastern counties of Pitt, Martin, Beaufort, and Craven apparently contemplated an organized uprising with the intention of gaining their freedom. Among the slaves who helped spread the word of the planned insurrection was Merrick, who belonged to Nathaniel Blinn of Bath. Whites uncovered and thwarted the plot, but not without the help of blacks, including a slave who belonged to Thomas Respess of Beaufort County.[27]

Housing Bath's Citizens

Houses in Bath were mostly unpretentious. They were frame, one-story buildings, described by William Logan in 1745 as "mean," which meant common or ordinary, or, more pejoratively, shabby or humble. They may well have been tarred rather than painted for preservation and accompanied by wooden, mud-daubed chimneys. Some may have been constructed on the hall-and-parlor plan. The hall or larger room served for family activities, including cooking and eating from wooden bowls, earthenware dishes, and pewter plates at a large table. The parlor, or smaller room, served for sleeping quarters and for private gatherings.

Cellars and lofts may have added space to otherwise small dwellings. In 1740 tavern keeper Edward Howcott purchased lots 5 and 6 in Bath on which stood a "Mansion House, with a brick chimney, one kitchen brick chimneyed, [and] one brick Store house & cellar," some of which may have dated from John Lawson's ownership and the founding of Bath.[28]

Without a doubt, however, the Palmer-Marsh House represented the architectural pièce de résistance in Bath. Built in 1751 by merchant-shipper Michael Coutanche, the house was the only private structure labeled on Sauthier's 1769 map of Bath. It occupied lots 24 and 25, and was constructed perpendicular to Main Street, a fashionable siting for southern colonial urban dwellings. The two-story house plus attic and cellar, based on a vernacular Georgian plan, measures twenty-five by fifty-one feet. The great summer beam that runs the length of the house reflects "the well-crafted solidarity of the dwelling," according to architectural historian Catherine Bishir. Beaded weatherboards cover the exterior, which is topped by a gable roof with eaves close to the house. A simple beading decorates door and window frames. Shutters flank the latter. The most notable feature of the house is a huge double stack, English bond, brick chimney on the east end of the building that rises from the large cooking fireplace in the cellar to a two-story brick pent. More than sixteen feet wide and four feet thick, it is double-shouldered with paved, sloped weatherings and corbelled top. The chimney encloses closets on the first and second stories whose windows are centered in the pent.[29]

The 1751 Palmer-Marsh House.

While Coutanche enjoyed the testament to his wealth until his death in 1761, the house soon passed from his family and ultimately became known as the Palmer-Marsh House. Robert Palmer, who succeeded Coutanche as Bath's wealthiest resident, bought the house in 1764 but apparently intended to sell it two years later, according to an advertisement in a Williamsburg, Virginia, newspaper: "To be Sold, at Bath town, in North Carolina, A Good Dwelling-House, two stories high, with four rooms on a floor, and a kitchen and cellars under the house." The advertisement was unsigned, but the description matched the Palmer-Marsh House. Palmer retained the house, however, until 1771, when he left Bath for New Bern, at which time he deeded the dwelling to his son William.[30]

Bath's Gathering Places — Taverns and Churches

In a new, frontier-like community such as Bath, peopled by competitive, ambitious men who sought to aggrandize property and acquire political preference, conflict often ensued. Unlike neighboring Virginia and South Carolina, North Carolina failed to develop a dominant socioeconomic elite, men who commanded respect in their governing role at both the local and provincial levels of politics. In Bath controversy swirled about Roger Kenyon, one of the town's early prominent citizens. In 1725 he accused former governor George Burrington of forcefully entering his house, threatening to burn the structure, and assaulting him with a stick. The following year one Charles Burroughs brought Kenyon into court on a charge of assault. In 1728 Kenyon took the offensive, first claiming that

To be SOLD, at Bath town, in North Carolina, A GOOD Dwelling-House, two stories high, with four rooms on a floor, and kitchen and cellars under the house; warehouses, wharf, and about 300 acres of good land adjoining the said town, very convenient for trade, or plantation business. Also three tracts of land, within three miles of the other; the greatest part of which is fine swamp land, easily drained, and a saw and grist mill on a very good stream, with 1100 acres of well timbered land running along the stream ten miles up the river. The terms will be left in writing at the said house for them together or separately, and the time of payment made convenient to any person (who takes all) with security. The purchaser may have such part of the furniture as may be agreed upon.   4

Advertisement in a Williamsburg newspaper for the sale of the Palmer-Marsh House, from the *Virginia Gazette*, July 25, 1766.

Matthew Rowan had spit in his face and attacked him with a stick, and then trading suits for defamation of character with blacksmith Andrew Frazier.[31]

Not surprisingly such incidents involved tavern keepers such as Roger Kenyon, or occurred in his establishment or others, for taverns were the most popular public gathering places in colonial America and often scenes of tumultuous behavior. The decision by the legislature in 1715 to require licensing of the establishments was motivated by a desire to find means "for the Better prevention of Riots and disorders in Ordinarys and other places where drink is retailed." But despite evidence of violence, excess, and immorality, taverns served an indispensable community role. In a society that depended greatly upon oral modes of communication, the social camaraderie and human interaction within the ordinary assumed a special significance, for that institution provided a prime medium for face-to-face confrontations by which men were cajoled, reasoned with, or intimidated. Moreover, opportunities for colonials to congregate elsewhere were few. Church gatherings were weekly affairs at best, and county courts met quarterly, but the tavern was open on a daily basis to all who wished to take advantage of its services.[32]

Tempering baser impulses was the impress of religion, more particularly that practiced by the Church of England or Anglican Church. The Carolina charters of 1663 and 1665, the Concessions and Agreement of 1665, and the Fundamental Constitutions of 1669 provided for the establishment of the Church of England in accordance with ecclesiastical laws of England, and for the erection of individual churches. At the same time the proprietors wanted to encourage immigration to their province. Thus the charters and governance documents permitted the toleration of dissenters, those who could not adhere in conscience to the Church of England. As a result the Society of Friends or Quakers, spurred by a brief visit in 1672 by George Fox, founder of the sect in England, emerged as the first element of organized religion in North Carolina, holding Monthly and Yearly Meetings by the end of the seventeenth century. Friends were confined principally to Perquimans and Pasquotank Precincts in the early eighteenth century. Few were found in Beaufort Precinct, though Quaker missionary Catherine Phillips held services at the courthouse in Bath in 1754.[33]

Although a petition from Anglicans in Beaufort Precinct in 1734 declared that "many sects and parties in Religion [have] settled amongst us," the number of dissenters in the vicinity of Bath was small and restricted to a scattering of Presbyterians, Baptists, and Roman Catholics. The original Huguenot settlers of Bath were few and elusive. They most likely succumbed to the Tuscarora in the war or intermarried with the English; one definitely moved on to South Carolina. Present in the colony perhaps as early as 1704, Presbyterians served by a minister had settled along the Neuse River in the mid-1720s. Yet their numbers were few until the substantial immigration in the 1730s of Scots and Scotch-Irish, most of whom settled in the Upper Cape Fear Valley and in the backcountry. Baptists appeared in the Albemarle as early as the 1690s and began to organize congregations in that region in the 1720s. They subsequently became quite numerous throughout the colony, but apparently their adherents were few around Bath. Naturalist and physician John Brickell, writing in 1731, declared that many Roman Catholics had settled in North Carolina, "mostly in and about Bath-Town," and that among them was a priest. Brickell probably exaggerated, although a decade later a reported twelve Catholics resided in the Anglican parish in which Bath was located. Still, dissenters were few; most in Bath and Beaufort Precinct who professed an attachment to religion supported the Church of England.[34]

Despite the early provision for the establishment of the Church of England in North Carolina, the Anglican Church was not recognized as the official church in the colony until the passage of several vestry acts and related legislation in 1701, 1703, 1708, and 1711. That early legislation divided North Carolina into parishes, including St. Thomas Parish, which included Pamtecough or Beaufort Precinct, in which Bath was located. During the formative years of the early eighteenth century, the vestry of St. Thomas Parish had little opportunity to advance the Anglican Church, especially considering the political turmoil and Indian war that engulfed the colony. Anglicans met for services in private residences, most notably that of Christopher Gale along Back Creek in Bath. Son of the Reverend Miles Gale, rector of Keighley Parish, Yorkshire, Gale opened his house to Anglicans on Sundays, "where a young gentleman, a lawyer, was appointed to read prayers and a sermon," according to a visiting Anglican minister.[35]

In the revisal of the laws in 1715, the General Assembly passed a new and expanded vestry act, modeled on the earlier legislation. The statute recognized St. Thomas Parish, which was made coterminous with Beaufort Precinct. The vestrymen for St. Thomas Parish named by the law were Gov. Charles Eden; Chief Justice Christopher Gale; Secretary Tobias Knight; Attorney General Daniel Richardson; Bath town commissioners Thomas Harding, John Porter, and John Drinkwater; and John Lillington, Thomas Worsley, John Adams, John Clarke, and Dr. Patrick Maule. The law, slightly revised by statute in 1741, made the vestries responsible for obtaining a minister, paying his salary, providing him with a glebe (residence and farmland for his support), and building a church or chapel for the parish.[36] In fact, most vestries in North Carolina fell far short of their legal directives and depended mainly upon the Society for the Propagation of the Gospel (SPG) to provide an Anglican ministry in the colony.

The SPG, founded in London in 1701 by the Reverend Dr. Thomas Bray, churchman and philanthropist, offered indispensable aid to the Church of England in the American colonies. The SPG attempted to provide missionaries for the colonies and to establish churches, libraries, and schools. It provided an annual salary to its missionaries, and furnished them with a small library and religious tracts for free distribution. Parishes were expected to furnish the balance of support for the missionaries. Between 1702 and 1783, the SPG sent 353 missionaries to America, including 33 of the 46 missionaries and rectors in North Carolina. Yet, North Carolina was inadequately served, for missionaries had to endure an uncongenial environment, marked by extreme difficulties of travel, physical privation, poverty, and unsupportive vestries and parishioners. Exacerbating these factors was the increasing presence of dissenters in the province and the general objection to the power of Anglican parishes to levy taxes.[37]

The Library at Bath

St. Thomas Parish and Bath benefited not only from the Anglican missionaries that were sent to North Carolina by the SPG, but also from Dr. Bray's attempt to establish parish libraries in America under the auspices of the Society for Promoting Christian Knowledge, which had been organized by 1699. As the Reverend Daniel Brett prepared to leave England for North Carolina on December 2, 1700, he was given a collection of books valued at £100 for "St. Thomas Parish in Pamlico in North Carolina." The minister apparently arrived safely in Bath County with the library in the early months of 1701 and proceeded to serve the Albemarle region as the first Anglican missionary in North Carolina. Unfortunately, Brett brought unspecified disgrace upon himself and embarrassment upon the Anglican Church, leading William Gale to describe him at his departure in 1703 as "ye Monster off [sic] ye Age."[38]

The library consisted of two separate collections. One was a parochial library for the use of the minister; the other, a layman's library for the use of the parishioners. The parochial library contained 153 titles in 176 volumes. Dr. Bray carefully selected the books to provide a minister in a frontier outpost with the sources necessary "to Instruct his people in all things necessary to Salvation." Thus the parochial library offered not only works of a religious nature but also titles that treated history, biography, natural sciences, medicine, geography, classical literature, poetry, heraldry, and sports. Bibles, commentaries, Latin and Greek lexicons, and dictionaries completed the collection. The layman's library contained 36 titles in 874 volumes, all of which dealt with religious topics. Most were tracts or pamphlets designed to be given away or loaned at the discretion of the minister. Only seven titles appeared in single volumes. Another seven were available in one hundred copies each, and the remainder in five to twenty copies each.[39]

Apparently the two libraries were combined upon their delivery to the parish, but the location, disposition, and dispersal of the books remain moot. Since the arrival of the library antedated the establishment of Bath, it must have been housed in a private home or homes in Pamtecough (Beaufort) Precinct. Eventually the volumes made their way to the town, perhaps to the house of Christopher Gale, son of an Anglican clergyman and staunch advocate of the church in North Carolina. Interestingly, one of the books in the library, *Opuscula Mythologica, Ethica et Physica*, was edited by Thomas Gale, Dean of York and uncle of Christopher Gale.[40]

Regardless of its location, the library evoked envy among Anglicans in the Albemarle, who contended not only that residents of Bath failed to appreciate its value but also that the books had originally been intended for Anglicans in the northern part of the province. Missionary Giles Rainsford complained in 1712 that "Dr. Bray's public library is all dispersed and lost by those wretches that don't consider the benefit of so valuable a gift." Two years later the vestry of St. Paul's Parish in Chowan Precinct wrote that by "an unhappy inscription on the Back of the Books or Title page," the library had been sent to St. Thomas Parish "in the then rising but now miserable County of Bath, falsely supposed to be the Seat of Government." On several occasions the Reverend John Urmstone, missionary in Chowan Precinct and surrounding areas from 1709 to 1721, bemoaned the misappropriation of the library, its misuse by Bath residents, and its expected demise. He blamed the "gentry of Bath" for making "waste paper of their Books rather than the clergy should have them, such is their esteem of our [ministerial] functions."[41]

Despite the protestations of Urmstone, Dr. Bray's library remained at its obviously intended destination, "St. Thomas Parish in Pamlico," and the General Assembly in 1715 moved to protect the collection of books. Legislation in that year designated self-perpetuating commissioners or trustees, including the governor, chief justice of the colony, and justices of the Beaufort Precinct Court, to oversee and preserve the library. The commissioners in turn were directed to appoint a "Library Keeper," who would catalogue the books, giving one list to the commissioners and one to the churchwardens of St. Thomas Parish. Loss of books except through unavoidable accidents subjected the library keeper to damages of twice their value. Upon the settlement of a minister in St. Thomas Parish, the minister automatically became the ex officio library keeper. Further, the law required that the library remain in the town of Bath, although with the approval of the commissioners the books might be taken to the house of the minister of the parish. The statute of 1715, aimed in part to "Secur[e] the Publick Library belonging to St. Thomas's Parish," proved the only law during the proprietary era to encourage literature, and the only law during the entire colonial era in North Carolina that addressed libraries.[42]

The General Assembly established a generous lending policy for the library. It permitted residents of Beaufort Precinct to borrow books (presumably from the layman's library) by giving a receipt to the library keeper, but required their return within one to four months, depending on the size of the volume. Since the law required the commissioners to meet annually on Easter Monday to inspect the library in order to confirm the presence of the books, the library keeper was instructed to ensure that all books were brought back ten days before that date. Failure to return volumes subjected the borrower to a penalty three times the value of the book or books. The law initially required the commissioners to appraise and establish a monetary value for each book.[43]

Although the legislation of 1715 strongly intimated that the library was basically intact at that time, and located in Bath, the ultimate disposition of the collection is unknown. Contemporary Anglican ministers hinted that poor care had been accorded the library, and Gov. George Burrington later declared that many of the volumes had been lost or destroyed even before 1715. Ultimately some of books may have been part of the library offered by Edward Moseley to the town of Edenton in 1723. However, historian Stephen B. Weeks concluded that the bulk of the Bath library remained together until midcentury, but by 1765 a contemporary source reported, "The books are mostly scattered and no library keeper [has] been appointed for many years." Apparently only one volume from the original Bath library has survived—Gabriel Towerson's *An Explication to the Catechism of the Church of England*, a folio edition printed in London in 1685. It surfaced in the Bath area in the 1880s and was given to the Diocese of East Carolina, which currently owns the volume.[44]

The Bath library represented one of at least thirty-nine libraries sent to America by the SPG and Dr. Bray before his death in 1739. Some, like the one at Bath, contained more than a thousand volumes. In addition, the SPG provided most of its missionaries in America with Bibles, prayer books, and theological works for their own use. However, according to historian Wilson Angley, Dr. Bray may have sent another substantial collection of books, a layman's library, to the Albemarle region (complementing the one sent to St. Thomas Parish) early in the eighteenth century. The contents of the Albemarle and St. Thomas Parish libraries were identical, and both were entrusted to the Reverend Daniel Brett in 1700 as he prepared to depart for North Carolina. When the Reverend Giles Rainsford wrote of the dispersal of Dr. Bray's library in 1712, he may well have referred to the Albemarle library, for the Bath library at that time seemed to have been fairly intact.[45]

St. Thomas Church

While the library remained a subject of controversy, the vestry of St. Thomas and Gov. Charles Eden, who made his home in Bath in 1716, sought the regular services of an Anglican missionary. The parish had probably been visited earlier by missionaries Daniel Brett, John Blair, and William Gordon. Subsequent to Eden's arrival, John Urmstone, Thomas Newman, and Thomas Bailey ministered to the inhabitants of Bath County. However, most, if not all, confined their labors principally to Albemarle County, visiting Bath County and St. Thomas Parish infrequently. Further, their tenure in North Carolina was usually brief, and the reputation of some was unenviable. Only upon the arrival in Bath of the Reverend John Garzia in 1734 did St. Thomas Parish obtain a minister of some permanence. At that time the churchwardens, vestry, and others in the parish petitioned the SPG to add Garzia to its list of missionaries in order that he might receive the customary annual stipend of £50 from the society, for they claimed they were "destitute of means . . . to allow a decent maintenance of a protestant Minister." The SPG complied in 1739, no doubt to the relief of Garzia, who had not been paid "his poor Salary . . . for two years and a half past," according to Gov. Gabriel Johnston.[46]

Garzia's appearance in St. Thomas Parish coincided with construction of St. Thomas Church in Bath, one of the first churches built in North Carolina and the oldest surviving church in the state. The legislation in 1715 that confirmed the establishment of the town of Bath and sought to protect Dr. Bray's library contained a provision that a church should be built in the town. Lot 61 was set aside for the structure, but the church was constructed about fifty feet north of its intended site, in the middle of what was supposed to be Craven Street. The alteration may have resulted from the encroachment of the original courthouse, slated for Lot 62, on Lot 61, which necessitated moving the site of the church. In any case the town commissioners had to add a strip of land to the church property to atone for the error. Construction of the church had begun by October 1734, under the auspices of churchwardens Simon Alderson, James Singleton, Charles Odeon, John Odeon, Thomas Jewell, William Willis, John Barrow, Robert Turner, and Edward Salter, and the walls and roof were finished by May 1735.[47]

In the beginning St. Thomas Church looked much as its does currently in its restored condition. Its relatively unsophisticated plan, a reflection no doubt of local builders, produced a plain, almost rectangular building of four bays constructed of (probably locally fired) brick laid in Flemish bond with glazed headers. The present (and presumably original) dimensions are nave length, fifty-one feet; nave width, thirty-one feet; nave height at the sides, fourteen feet; and wall thickness, two feet. The original church may have featured a hipped roof, which would have been highly unusual for any building in early North Carolina, though not for Anglican churches in Maryland. In fact, brick churches in North Carolina, including St. Paul's in Edenton and St. Philips in Brunswick Town, as well as St. Thomas, bore a far more striking resemblance to those in Maryland than to churches in neighboring Virginia and South Carolina. St. Thomas originally may also have possessed a tower or steeple, a common element in both Virginia and Maryland churches.[48]

St. Thomas at its completion was the only church in North Carolina in which Anglican services were held and proved to be one of only a few churches built by the Church of England before the Revolution. Construction was soon begun on St. Paul's Church in Edenton, though many years elapsed before it was finished, and Anglican churches appeared later in Wilmington and Brunswick Town. The Reverend John Garzia continued to serve St. Thomas Parish until his death in 1744, which was occasioned by a fall from his horse. Briefly joining Garzia was the famed English itinerant George Whitefield, whose preaching sparked the outburst of the revival in the colonies known as the Great Awakening. Arriving in Bath in December 1739, Whitefield spoke to an audience of approximately one hundred persons, perhaps in the church, though possibly outside in the open air. Despite the presence of Garzia, Whitefield remarked that his listeners had suffered from "a famine of the Word among them for a long while," perhaps because as Whitefield later contended, Garzia could "scarce speak English."[49]

However, by all accounts Garzia was capable and devoted, though his parishioners repaid his efforts with a spirit of ingratitude. In his words, "adultery,

Itinerant English preacher George Whitefield visited Bath intermittently during the 1730s and 1740s.

Incest, Blasphemy, and all kinds of profaneness" had taken "deep root" in his parish, while the vestry endeavored "to hinder and obstruct the Service of God, . . . as much as possible [dissuaded] others from it[,] and . . . in a particular manner exercise[d] their malice daily against me, by depriving me of my quietness of mind and enjoyment of . . . [my] small Salary." After Garzia's death, his widow Mary and children lived in abject poverty in Bath. An Anglican missionary wrote in 1751 that Mary Garzia had "sold almost all her goods out of mere necessity for subsistence, . . . and was in danger of having her Bed taken from under her." As late as 1760 the Reverend Alexander Stewart informed the SPG that she was "really an Object of Charity." At that time, as it had earlier, the SPG offered Mrs. Garzia a small sum for assistance.[50]

Following the demise of the Reverend John Garzia, Whitefield again visited St. Thomas Parish in the 1740s, referring to the area as "ungospelized wilds." Not until 1753 did the parish obtain the services of a settled minister—the Reverend Alexander Stewart. Although beset by family losses and poor health, the Reverend Mr. Stewart labored tirelessly on behalf of St. Thomas Parish and the surrounding area, which included present Hyde and Pitt Counties. He served St. Thomas Church and thirteen scattered chapels. In addition to ministering to whites, Rev. Alexander Stewart arguably more than any other Anglican missionary in North Carolina tried to spread the gospel among African Americans, as well as among the remnants of scattered Indian tribes in Hyde County. Stewart also found time to write *Validity of Infant Baptism*, a defense of infant baptism to confound the Anabaptists, which was published in 1758 by James Davis in New Bern. Additionally, Stewart persuaded the SPG to send him a Bible and a Book of Common Prayer for the use of the church, and a number of books and pamphlets for a "Missionary's Library," in effect partially reestablishing on a small scale the original library sent to St. Thomas Parish by the SPG in 1700.[51]

Meanwhile the parish repaired St. Thomas Church and provided a glebe for the Reverend Mr. Stewart. The church had fallen into a "very ruinous" condition following the death of Garzia, but repairs were made after the arrival of Stewart, and services were conducted on a regular basis at the end of 1754. However, by 1765 the structure again needed "considerable repairs."[52] In addition to maintaining the church, the parish established the first Anglican glebe in North Carolina. At the time of the incorporation of Bath, land had been set aside for a glebe for Anglican ministers, and provincial legislation later required Anglican parishes to provide land and a house to support their ministers. But the parishes were dilatory, and not until 1763 did Stewart report, "I am now living in the 1st Glebe House ever finished in this Province." The minister later added that he had agreed to clear and improve twenty-five acres of land and contribute £40 towards the construction of the house. The glebe apparently was located immediately

St. Thomas Episcopal Church, built in 1734, the oldest extant church in North Carolina.

upstream from Bath on the opposite side of Bath Creek across from Ferry Point. Stewart occupied the house for about two years after which he purchased a plantation on Durham's Creek to use as his principal residence.[53]

Before succumbing to an undisclosed illness in 1771, Stewart had been assisted by Peter Blinn of Bath, a representative of the town in the House of Commons, a justice of the peace of Beaufort County, and commissioner of customs for the Port of Bath. In 1769 Blinn journeyed to London to seek ordination, carrying with him letters of recommendation from Stewart and William Tryon, governor of North

Carolina. Successful in his mission, Blinn returned to North Carolina, only to die soon thereafter in 1770. Whether he officiated at St. Thomas Church is unknown. The last to serve St. Thomas Parish and the surrounding area before the Revolution was the Reverend Nathaniel Blount, who was born in Beaufort County. Possibly influenced by Stewart to turn to the ministry, Blount sailed to England in 1773 for ordination, buttressed by a glowing recommendation from the vestry of St. Thomas Parish, which clearly hoped to secure his services. The last Anglican clergyman ordained for service in North Carolina, Blount labored tirelessly for the Anglican Church, renamed the Protestant Episcopal Church after the Revolution.[54]

Education and Communication

In addition to their spiritual responsibilities, the ministers of the Anglican Church assumed a prominent role in providing institutionalized education to the North Carolina populace. The first known schoolteacher in the colony was Charles Griffin, a lay reader of the Anglican Church who opened a school near Nixonton in Pasquotank Precinct in 1705. As settlement expanded, so did the number of schools. Anglican missionary James Moir taught in Brunswick County in 1745, and the Reverend Daniel Earl, rector of St. Paul's Parish in Chowan, opened a school at his home near Edenton in the 1750s. Efforts to educate African Americans derived principally from Dr. Bray's Associates, an English philanthropic organization that worked through the Anglican Church to bring religious instruction to young blacks. The Associates apparently considered erecting schools in the Cape Fear, Albemarle, and Bath areas. Although the Associates' efforts in the Cape Fear and the Albemarle were futile, with their aid the Reverend Alexander Stewart of St. Thomas Parish opened a school in Hyde County in the 1760s in which the schoolmaster and schoolmistress taught a small number of African Americans and Native Americans.[55]

Many nonsectarian public and private schools offered educational opportunities to the youth of North Carolina. A wealthy individual, a group of neighboring families, or an aspiring teacher might instigate a school. At least two individuals in colonial North Carolina provided endowments in their wills for free schools, James Winwright of Carteret County in 1744 and James Innes of New Hanover County in 1760. Moreover, provincial law required orphaned boys and girls with sufficient estates to be placed with guardians who would educate and provide for the children "according to their Rank & degree." Poor orphans were apprenticed to learn a handicraft or trade and at the same time to read, write, and sometimes "cypher." Most county courts instructed masters to give their apprentices from one to two years of schooling. A reference in Beaufort County deeds in 1742 to an "old School house," and the presence in 1754 of schoolmaster James Willcocks suggest at least limited opportunities in the county, if not in the town of Bath, to acquire the rudiments of learning. When private or free schools were unavailable, children might receive instruction from parents, older siblings, tutors, and itinerant schoolmasters.[56]

Education, of course, encompassed more than academic instruction. Wyriot Ormond (son of Wyriot Ormond), by his will in 1773, warned his executors that no expense was too great for the education of his two daughters. He added, "I not only mean that part of their Education which Respects their Schooling, but Every Other that Can be had for their Advantage," presumably instruction in the ability to dress properly, converse discreetly, and manage a household skillfully. Education broadly understood also embodied interest in and access to the world beyond the immediate locale of the colonials. The tradition of southern hospitality stemmed in part from the desire for good conversation and news. Hosts plied their visitors for the latest inter-colonial and international developments. Curiosity, a marked characteristic of lower-class American colonials that occasionally bordered on impertinence, reflected a desire for information about the external world. Written communications consisted principally of letters and newspapers, though the latter were few in North Carolina. Only four newspapers were published in the colony before the Revolution, two in New Bern and two in Wilmington.[57]

Impeding the flow of information was the lack of an adequate postal system, though Bath's location on the principal thoroughfare through North Carolina placed the town in a favorable position to take advantage of the mail facilities that eventually materialized. An effort in 1739 to establish a post in North Carolina, using the coastal highway through Bath to link Virginia and South Carolina, failed. As a result North Carolinians continued to depend upon friends, expresses (private carriers), and packet boats in the coastal trade to transport letters and papers. Only the assiduous efforts of Gov. William Tryon brought a permanent post to fruition in North Carolina in 1770, finally closing the last gap in the provincial postal system along the Atlantic coast from New England to Georgia. The route followed the north-south coastal highway through North Carolina, linking Suffolk, Virginia to Georgetown, South Carolina, via Edenton, Bath, New Bern, Wilmington, and Brunswick Town, a distance of approximately 377 miles that took twenty-four days to traverse.[58]

The postal service was slow and inefficient. Deliveries were made every two weeks between Edenton and New Bern through Bath. Riders were often delayed by the difficult ferriages over the Albemarle Sound and the Pamlico and Neuse Rivers (as well as the Trent, New, and Cape Fear Rivers to the south). Postmasters in the towns were unreliable and did not maintain regular post offices. Letters were carelessly tossed on tables or floors with no regard for security of the correspondence. Frequently other parties opened the mail. British postal inspector Hugh Finlay in 1774 found that William Brown, postmaster in Bath, maintained shoddy accounts, never keeping a book, but putting "his accounts of receipts of Postage on scraps of

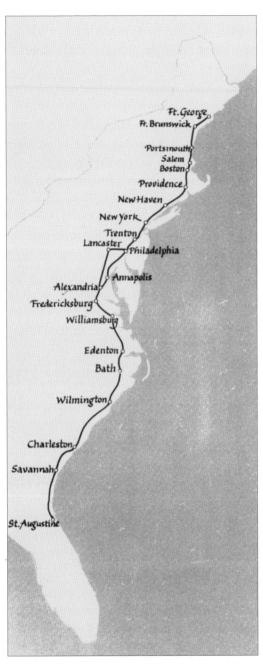

Route of the colonial post road.

Paper." At the same time Brown charged £46 sterling per annum for his services, a startlingly high sum that exceeded postal receipts in Bath. Brown refused to accept less, preferring to relinquish his job. Finding a reliable replacement would have been extremely difficult. Thus for Bath, and for the entire colony, communication with the external world remained infrequent and unreliable.[59]

At the time when a permanent post was established in North Carolina, Bath remained a small but bustling community. As Bath was the seat of Beaufort County, the sheriff and clerk of the county court kept their offices there to serve the needs of the people. Quarterly meetings of the county court brought throngs of area residents to town on public business. Because Bath was also the seat of the customs district of Port Bath, all ships trading to the area, or, at least, their captains, had to enter and clear with the customs commissioners in the town. Those who lived in Beaufort and surrounding counties who wanted to purchase land from the Crown had to visit Bath for that purpose, at least while Robert Palmer was the entry taker for royal lands and living in Bath. Adding to the influx of visitors were worshipers at St. Thomas Church on Sundays. Homes, stores, and taverns offered various entertainments, all augmented in the mid-1770s by the wartime excitement. On successive evenings in 1777, Ebenezer Hazard found sufficient diversion to remain in town until two o'clock in the morning before retiring to the plantation of Richard N. Stephens, with whom he was staying. At that point Bath had reached its peak of prominence, for the postwar years found the town assuming the role of a quiet community whose colonial history constituted its principal legacy.[60]

NOTES

1. Clark, *State Records*, 25:193; Saunders, *Colonial Records*, 4:833.

2. Saunders, *Colonial Records*, 2:143-144; John Brickell, *The Natural History of North Carolina* (1737; reprint, Murfreesboro, N.C.: Johnson Publishing Company, 1968), 8; "William Logan's Journal," 10; Johnston, "Journal of Ebenezer Hazard," 370; Cain, *Records of the Executive Council, 1735-1754*, xxxvii.

3. George Whitefield, *George Whitefield's Journals (1737-1741)* (Gainesville, Fla.: Scholars' Facsimiles and Reprints, 1969), 375, 377.

4. Whitefield, *Journals*, 375-376; Johnston, "Journal of Ebenezer Hazard," 370-372; Hugh Finlay, *Journal Kept by Hugh Finlay, Surveyor of the Post Roads on the Continent of North America* (Brooklyn: Frank H. Norton, 1867), 86; Elkanah Watson, *Men and Times of the Revolution; or Memoirs of Elkanah Watson*, ed. Winslow C. Watson (New York: Dana and Company, 1856), 38; "Journal of a French Traveller," 736; Smyth, *Tour*, 2:100; Henry Mouzon Map, 1775, copy, State Archives, Office of Archives and History, Raleigh.

5. Johann David Schoepf, *Travels in the Confederation, 1783-1784*, trans. and ed. Alfred J. Morrison, 2 vols. (Philadelphia: William J. Campbell, 1911), 1:118-119; Alan D. Watson, "The Ferry in Colonial North Carolina: A Vital Link in Transportation," *North Carolina Historical Review* 51 (summer 1974): 249-266.

6. Whitefield, *Journals*, 377; "William Logan's Journal," 10; "Journal of a French Traveller," 736; Watson, *Men and Times of the Revolution*, 38; Clark, *State Records*, 23:149-150.

7. Beaufort County Court Minutes, September term 1756, September term 1759; "Journal of a French Traveller," 736; Johnston, "Journal of Ebenezer Hazard," 371 and n. 59; Watson, *Men and Times of the Revolution*, 38; Finlay, *Journal*, 86.

8. A pirate community was organized on the basis of democratic principles by which captains, directions of cruises, and the choice of taking a prize were determined by majority vote. According to historian Marcus Rediker, pirates created "a rough, improvised, but effective egalitarianism that placed authority in the collective hands of the crew." In addition, members of a pirate crew signed an agreement among themselves known as "the articles," a set of rules governing their conduct, the distribution of prize money, and the care of disabled comrades. Clearly the existence of those flying the *Jolly Roger* differed markedly from that of ordinary merchant seamen. Lindley S. Butler, *Pirates, Privateers, and Rebel Raiders of the Carolina Coast* (Chapel Hill: University of North Carolina Press, 2000), 7-10; Marcus Rediker, " 'Under the Banner of King Death': The Social World of Anglo-American Pirates, 1716-1726," *William and Mary Quarterly* [3d ser.] 38 (April 1981): 209. See also Hugh F. Rankin, *The Pirates of Colonial North Carolina*, rev. ed. (Raleigh: Division of Archives and History, Department of Cultural Resources, 2001); Marcus Rediker, *Between the Devil and the Deep Blue Sea: Merchant Seamen, Pirates, and the Anglo-American Maritime World, 1700-1750* (Cambridge: Cambridge University Press, 1987).

9. Butler, *Pirates, Privateers, and Rebel Raiders*, 29-39; David Moore, "Blackbeard the Pirate: Historical Background and the Beaufort Inlet Shipwrecks," *Tributaries* 7 (1997): 31-36; Rankin, *Pirates of Colonial North Carolina*, 53-61.

10. Butler, *Pirates, Privateers, and Rebel Raiders*, 40-42; Rankin, *Pirates of Colonial North Carolina*, 51-53; Robert J. Cain, ed., *Records of the Executive Council, 1664-1734*, vol. 7 of *The Colonial Records of North Carolina [Second Series]* (Raleigh: Division of Archives and History, Department of Cultural Resources, 1984), 80.

11. Moore, "Blackbeard the Pirate," 34-38; Butler, *Pirates, Privateers, and Rebel Raiders*, 25-29, 42-49; Price, *North Carolina Higher-Court Records, 1709-1723*, xxxiii; Cain, *Records of the Executive Council, 1664-1734*, 83-89.

12. Book 1, pp. 216-217 (microfilm), Beaufort County Deeds; Reed, *Beaufort County*, 49; "Charles Eden," in Powell, *Dictionary of North Carolina Biography*, 2:134. Eden also owned lots 9, 10, 67, and 68. Book 1, p. 231 (microfilm), Beaufort County Deeds.

13. Book 1, pp. 53, 54 (microfilm), Beaufort County Deeds; Reed, *Beaufort County*, 47-48; "Christopher Gale," in Powell, *Dictionary of North Carolina Biography*, 2:260-264.

14. Book 1, pp. 251, 388, 411-412, 451-453 (microfilm), Beaufort County Deeds; Price, *North Carolina Higher-Court Records, 1709-1723*, 291; Cain, *North Carolina Higher-Court Records, 1724-1730*, 446-447; Cheney, *North Carolina Government*, 1057.

15. Book 2, pp. 36-37 (microfilm), Beaufort County Deeds; Saunders, *Colonial Records*, 3:123; Price, "'Men of Good Estates,'" 79; "Matthew Rowan," in Powell, *Dictionary of North Carolina Biography*, 5:258. Rowan may well have left Bath as early as 1728, for in that year he appointed Edward Salter to act as his attorney. Book 1, p. 553 (microfilm), Beaufort County Deeds.

16. Book 2, pp. 331, 347-348, 381-382, 534-535; Book 3, pp. 126-127, 177 (microfilm), Beaufort County Deeds; Cheney, *North Carolina Government*, 1057; Peter B. Sandbeck, "Dendrochronology: A New Tool for Dating Historic Structures," *Tributaries* 2 (1992): 29; Jerry L. Cross, "The Palmer- Marsh House," (report, Research Branch, Division of Archives and History, August 1976), no pagination.

17. Wilson Angley, "A History of St. Thomas Episcopal Church, Bath, North Carolina" (report, Research Branch, Division of Archives and History, Raleigh, February 1981), 62-78; "Alexander Stewart," in Powell, *Dictionary of North Carolina Biography*, 5:447-448; Saunders, *Colonial Records*, 8:159-160; David M. Ludlum, *Early American Hurricanes, 1492-1870* (Boston: American Meteorological Society, 1963), 49.

18. "The Memorial of Robert Palmer[,] Surveyor Gen[era]l of the Lands in No[rth] Carol[ina,] One of His Majesty's Council and late Collector of the Port of Bath Town," December 30, 1783, Audit Office, 12/36, 41-42, 46 (microfilm), State Archives, Office of Archives and History, Raleigh; Book 4, pp. 348-350 (microfilm), Beaufort County Deeds; Clark, *State Records*, 11:155-156; Cheney, *North Carolina Government*, 1057; Reed, *Beaufort County*, 94; Cross, "Palmer-Marsh House."

19. Watson, *Men and Times of the Revolution*, 252; "Journal of a French Traveller," 736; "Journal of Josiah Quincy, Junior, 1773," Massachusetts Historical Society *Proceedings* 49 (1916): 461; Saunders, *Colonial Records*, 8:272.

20. "Memorial of Robert Palmer," 43-46; Clark, *State Records*, 24:424-425; Reed, *Beaufort County*, 94; Cross, "Palmer-Marsh House." Sources differ over the date of Palmer's death. One claims that he died ca. 1790; another, in 1802. See "Robert Palmer," in Powell, *Dictionary of North Carolina Biography*, 5:13; Reed, *Beaufort County*, 94.

21. Beaufort County Tax List, 1755, Treasurer's and Comptroller's Papers, State Archives, Office of Archives and History, Raleigh; Cain, *North Carolina Higher-Court Records, 1724-1730*, 27-28; Alan D. Watson, "Household Size and Composition in Pre-Revolutionary North Carolina," *Mississippi Quarterly* 31 (fall 1978): 569.

22. Book 1, pp. 221, 226-227; Book 2, pp. 61-62, 168, 360-361 (microfilm), Beaufort County Deeds.

23. Joe A. Mobley, ed., *The Way We Lived in North Carolina* (Chapel Hill: University of North Carolina Press, 2003), 35; Jeffrey J. Crow, Paul D. Escott, and Flora J. Hatley, *A History of African Americans in North Carolina*, rev. ed. (Raleigh: Office of Archives and History, Department of Cultural Resources, 2002), 2.

24. Beaufort County Tax List, 1755; Saunders, *Colonial Records*, 9:804; Watson, "Household Size and Composition," 564.

25. Catherine Phillips, *Memories of the Life of Catherine Phillips: To Which Are Added Some of Her Epistles* (Philadelphia: Budd and Bartram, 1797), 92.

26. Magistrates and Freeholders Courts, 1715-1793, Secretary of State Papers, State Archives, Office of Archives and History, Raleigh.

27. Saunders, *Colonial Records*, 10:94; Jeffrey J. Crow, *The Black Experience in Revolutionary North Carolina* (Raleigh: Division of Archives and History, Department of Cultural Resources, 1977), 55-61; Alan D. Watson, "Impulse Toward Independence: Resistance and Rebellion among North Carolina Slaves, 1750-1775," *Journal of Negro History* 63 (fall 1978): 319-326.

28. "William Logan's Journal," 9-10; Catherine W. Bishir, Charlotte V. Brown, Carl R. Lounsbury, and Ernest H. Wood III, *Architects and Builders in North Carolina: A History of the Practice of Building* (Chapel Hill: University of North Carolina Press, 1990), 20; Book 2, p. 345 (microfilm), Beaufort County Deeds.

29. Sauthier map of Bath, 1769; Sandbeck, "Dendrochronology," 29; Catherine W. Bishir, *North Carolina Architecture* (Chapel Hill: University of North Carolina Press, 1990), 16; Marilyn Dee Castro, "Historical Houses of Beaufort County, North Carolina, 1744-1899" (Ph.D. diss., University of North Carolina at Greensboro, 1982), 52-55; Cross, "Palmer-Marsh House."

30. *Virginia Gazette* (Purdie and Dixon) (Williamsburg), July 25, 1766; Cross, "Palmer-Marsh House." Given Coutanche's political presence, coupled with the impressiveness of the new structure, the Palmer-Marsh House may well have been used for some public function during the 1752 legislative session held at Bath, as local tradition suggests.

31. Cain, *North Carolina Higher-Court Records, 1724-1730*, 220, 228, 271-272, 446-449.

32. Clark, *State Records*, 23:80; Watson, "Colonial Tavern," 41.

33. Robert J. Cain, ed. *The Church of England in North Carolina: Documents, 1699-1741*, vol. 10 of *The Colonial Records of North Carolina [Second Series]*(Raleigh: Division of Archives and History, Department of Cultural Resources, 1999), xiii-xxi; Cain, *Records of the Executive Council, 1735-1754*, li; Seth B. Hinshaw, *The Carolina Quaker Experience, 1665-1985* (Greensboro, N.C.: Friends Historical Society, 1984); David Cecelski, *A Historian's Coast: Adventures into the Tidewater Past* (Winston-Salem: John Blair, 2000): 12-14.

34. Brickell, *Natural History*, 36; Cain, *North Carolina Higher-Court Records, 1724-1730*, xxxv-xxxvi; Angley, "History of St. Thomas Episcopal Church," 36.

35. Saunders, *Colonial Records*, 1:80; Cain, *Church of England in North Carolina*, xxi, xxiii-xxxi.

36. Clark, *State Records*, 23:6-10, 187-191; Joseph Blount Cheshire, ed., *Sketches of Church History in North Carolina* (Wilmington, N.C.: William L. DeRosset Jr., 1892), 64.

37. Angley, "History of St. Thomas Episcopal Church," 3-4; Sarah McCulloh Lemmon, "The Genesis of the Protestant Episcopal Diocese of North Carolina, 1701-1823," *North Carolina Historical Review* 28 (October 1951): 433-435, 442-445; Watson, *Society in Colonial North Carolina*, 86, 88.

38. Clark, *State Records*, 22:733; Angley, "History of St. Thomas Episcopal Church," 14. Interestingly, although all sources indicate that North Carolina's first vestry act was passed in 1701,

in December 1700 the Reverend Daniel Brett was given books for St. Thomas Parish in North Carolina. See Cain, *Church of England in North Carolina*, xxiv, 22.

39. Paschal, *History of Colonial Bath*, 12-13. See generally John Kenneth Gibson, "Thomas Bray Libraries, St. Thomas Parish, Pamlico (Bath, North Carolina), 1700: A Bibliographical and Historical Analysis" (master's thesis, University of North Carolina, 1986).

40. Saunders, *Colonial Records*, 1:715; Angley, "History of St. Thomas Episcopal Church," 17.

41. Saunders, *Colonial Records*, 1:860; 2:118-120, 130-132.

42. Clark, *State Records*, 23:76-78; Stephen B. Weeks, "Libraries and Literature in North Carolina in the Eighteenth Century," in *Annual Report of the American Historical Association, 1895* (Washington, D.C.: Government Printing Office, 1896), 179-180.

43. Clark, *State Records*, 23:77-78.

44. Saunders, *Colonial Records*, 3:187; Weeks, "Libraries and Literature in North Carolina," 192; Angley, "History of St. Thomas Episcopal Church," 23-24.

45. Saunders, *Colonial Records*, 1:860; Angley, "History of St. Thomas Episcopal Church," 24-25.

46. Angley, "History of St. Thomas Episcopal Church," 27-37. In 1735 Garzia purchased lots 49, 50, and 51 in the northeastern corner of town. Book 2, pp. 172-173 (microfilm), Beaufort County Deeds.

47. Clark, *State Records*, 23:73; Angley, "History of St. Thomas Episcopal Church," 38-39.

48. Angley, "History of St. Thomas Episcopal Church," 43-45, 49-53.

49. Angley, "History of St. Thomas Episcopal Church," 54-55.

50. Angley, "History of St. Thomas Episcopal Church," 55-59.

51. Paschal, *History of Colonial Bath*, 47; Angley, "History of St. Thomas Episcopal Church," 62-68.

52. Saunders, *Colonial Records*, 7:102-104; Angley, "History of St. Thomas Episcopal Church," 70-71.

53. Lawson, *New Voyage to Carolina*, 171; Saunders, *Colonial Records*, 6:996; 7:495-496; Angley, "History of St. Thomas Episcopal Church," 71-74. Although John Lawson early claimed that the glebe land was contiguous to Bath, it probably lay across the creek, according to historian Wilson Angley.

54. Sarah McCulloh Lemmon, "Nathaniel Blount: Last Clergyman of the 'Old Church,'" *North Carolina Historical Review* 50 (autumn 1973): 351-356; Reed, *Beaufort County*, 139; Angley, "History of St. Thomas Episcopal Church," 78-83.

55. Robert J. Cain, ed., *Records of the Executive Council, 1755-1775*, vol. 9 of *The Colonial Records of North Carolina [Second Series]* (Raleigh: Division of Archives and History, Department of Cultural Resources, 1994), xxxi-xxxii; Watson, *Society in Colonial North Carolina*, 70-71, 73.

56. Book 2, p. 408; Book 3, p. 175 (microfilm), Beaufort County Deeds; Watson, *Society in Colonial North Carolina*, 71-73.

57. J. Bryan Grimes, ed., *North Carolina Wills and Inventories* (Raleigh: Edwards and Broughton Printing Company, 1912), 324; Watson, *Society in Colonial North Carolina*, 108-109.

58. *Virginia Gazette*, May 25, 1739; *South Carolina Gazette* (Charleston), April 26, 1739; Finlay, *Journal*, 88; Charles Christopher Crittenden, "Means of Communication in North Carolina, 1763-1789," *North Carolina Historical Review* 8 (October 1931): 373-376.

59. Finlay, *Journal*, 85; Crittenden, "Means of Communication," 376-378.

60. Johnston, "Journal of Ebenezer Hazard," 370-371; Reed, *Beaufort County*, 94.

Epilogue: The Second and Third Centuries

The American Revolution marked the advent of a new nation but simultaneously witnessed the decline of the significance of Bath. On the eve of independence, James Bonner undertook the development of the town of Washington on the Pamlico River about fifteen miles above Bath. From its inception in 1775-1776, when Bonner began to sell lots on the north bank of the river, Washington apparently became a center of commerce. Since it was located upstream from Bath, Washington was better situated to secure the Pamlico River trade, an advantage recognized by several Bath residents who numbered among Washington's early merchants. The General Assembly in 1782 incorporated Washington. Three years later the legislature, adverting to the inconvenient geographic location of Bath and the ruinous condition of the courthouse, transferred the seat of Beaufort County from Bath to Washington, dealing a crushing blow to the prospects of the older town.[1]

Meanwhile Bath, given its status as a port and established town, played a role of minor importance during the Revolution. The provisional government of North Carolina in 1776 authorized the purchase of kettles in Bath for making salt for the Continental army. That same year a cannon that had been shipped to Bath was sent to Edenton and four years later muskets arrived in the port from St. Eustatia in the West Indies. Despite this small flurry of activity, Bath's place as a viable port was considerably diminished. While approximately thirty ships a year entered Bath in the mid-eighteenth century, this number had dropped to seven or eight by the 1770s.[2] Bath also served as a recruitment center for the Patriot army; in 1778 Thomas Bonner led twenty-one men into service from the town to Halifax. Although North Carolina's long coastline was virtually unprotected, and the British navy blockaded Ocracoke Inlet and on occasion landed forces on the Outer Banks, Bath and the interior sound region were never seriously threatened.[3]

The Economic Decline of Bath

The meteoric rise of Washington as a port and county seat relegated Bath to the small community that it was destined to remain. In 1786 tax records listed only 13 lots in Bath as "improved," while 42½ were "unimproved." After the Revolution travelers, including President George Washington on his Southern Tour in 1791, began to bypass Bath in order to avoid the lengthy ferriages across the Albemarle Sound and Pamlico River, preferring to travel from Virginia to New Bern by way of Halifax, Tarboro, or Washington. At the same time, shipping in the Port Bath District gravitated to Washington. Nathan Keais, collector of Port Bath, maintained his residence and office in Washington after the mid-1780s. By 1790, the shipping district had been renamed Port Washington and the town of Washington designated the sole port of entry for the district by the federal government. Bath's continued decline was evident on William Latham's 1807 map, showing Bath as having only seven buildings, and on R. H. B. Brazier's 1828 map, depicting but four houses in the town.[4]

As Bath receded in the shadow of Washington, several houses from the eighteenth and early nineteenth centuries, including the Palmer-Marsh House and the Van Der Veer House, reflected the wealth and sophistication of the older town.

The Van Der Veer House.

As mentioned above the former, built by Michael Coutanche and subsequently owned by Robert Palmer and his son William, passed to the Marsh family. Jonathan Marsh, a native of Rhode Island, leased the house in 1795 and purchased it seven years later. The house remained in the Marsh family until 1915.

The Van Der Veer House was built in the mid- to late 1790s. Probably constructed by Dr. Ephraim Whitmore, the two-story, three-bay frame structure topped by a gambrel roof became the property of Joseph Bonner, which he retained for one day before selling it to Jacob Van Der Veer, his business partner. Van Der Veer arrived in Bath from New Jersey and operated a ropewalk north of the town limits. He altered the house significantly during his twelve-year residence. Charles W. Bowen, a subsequent owner, in turn extensively remodeled the structure in the 1920s.[5]

Joseph Bonner—businessman, planter, and briefly owner of the Van Der Veer House—prospered in Bath. He moved his family from Washington to Bath in 1824. Among his properties were the Jackson Swamp plantation (formerly owned by the Palmers) north of town, a steam sawmill on Bath Creek, and land at the end of Main Street overlooking the confluence of Bath and Back Creeks, formerly owned by John Lawson. Here, about 1830, Bonner erected the house that currently bears his name. The two-story, side-hall-plan house with a one-story wing features a double-shouldered Flemish bond chimney. According to tradition, the Bonner

The Bonner House.

House, or portions of it, were constructed from materials salvaged from shipwrecks on the Outer Banks, but most likely the lumber came from Bonner's sawmill at the other end of Main Street.[6]

Bonner and his family worshiped at St. Thomas Church, which survives as Bath's oldest extant structure. Following its collapse in North Carolina after the Revolution, the Protestant Episcopal Church, formerly the Church of England, eventually revived. In 1823, six years after the formation of the Diocese of North Carolina, St. Thomas Church was formally accepted into the diocese, and in 1824 Bishop John Starke Ravenscroft visited the church. A Sunday school was instituted in 1831 but languished for want of teachers and interest. About 1840 a severe storm destroyed the roof and gable ends of the building. The restoration, led by Joseph Bonner, took many years. As a result of impoverished circumstances and the occasional absences of ministerial appointees, the number of communicants at St. Thomas fluctuated considerably. By the eve of the Civil War, membership had stabilized at thirty under the Reverend Israel Harding. At that time, monthly services at the church reportedly were well attended.[7]

During the antebellum era, the Episcopalians in Bath faced competition from Methodists. The Methodists organized in the town early in the nineteenth century, perhaps in the 1820s, and during the 1830s held services in a small frame church on Carteret Street. About 1840 they replaced that church with another built behind the Palmer-Marsh House. This structure served as a school for many years before it was demolished. In 1844 Bath was the scene of a revival, presumably Methodist, the first held in twenty, perhaps forty, years, according to one participant. The present Methodist Church, erected in 1891, although probably not finished for another three years, stands on South Main Street.[8]

Between the early 1830s and 1850s, tax records for the town of Bath show that the valuations of town lots declined as trade continued to flourish in Washington. The town's population during the same period was predominantly African American, with taxable black males outnumbering taxable white males three or four to one.[9] In 1837, for example, there were 66 white and 225 black polls listed in the Bath tax district.[10] Although the majority of those African Americans were enslaved and may have been working on plantations outside of town, the character of Bath's streets in the mid-nineteenth century would have been predominantly African American.

Although figures cannot be determined specifically for Bath, free blacks comprised a very small percentage of the Beaufort County African American population throughout the eighteenth century and the first half of the nineteenth. The 1790 federal census listed 5,462 people in Beaufort County; of those individuals enumerated, 1,632 were enslaved and 129 were non-white free persons.[11] By 1810, free blacks numbered between 100 and 300, and in 1830, between 300 and 500. Like the family of Gabriel Blango, who first appeared in the 1800 census, many of Beaufort County's free blacks seem to have lived in Washington. In 1830, twelve free blacks in Beaufort County owned slaves.[12] In no instance did any of those individuals possess more than four slaves; several of the slave owners were women.

At mid-nineteenth century, Bath for a short time appeared to be a thriving community. In 1850, the town staged a celebration of the anniversary of national independence on July 4. At that time two hotels attested to the presence of numerous visitors. A school or "academy" in 1850-1851 offered instruction to boys and girls, including a regimen of study for young men preparing for college. Ephraim Willis operated a marine railway where he built and repaired small sailing vessels and flatboats. Farmers of the county chose Bath as the location for inaugurating the Beaufort County Agricultural Society in 1851. The town was an understandable choice, since in 1852-1853, Dr. John M. Tompkins, a leading agriculturalist, published the *Farmer's Journal* there before he moved to Raleigh to continue the agricultural newspaper. Yet a few years later, a palpable malaise swept Bath, leading one individual who lived in the town to bemoan the removal of several friends. A former resident remarked, "I never saw a place go down like it has in my life. To tell the truth I do not think there is [*sic*] but three good looking houses in the place."[13]

The Civil War added to the distress of Bath. Less than a year after the outbreak of the conflict, United States troops made their appearance in Beaufort County. After the fall of New Bern in March 1862, Federal soldiers took possession of Washington. Although spared the horrors of battle, Bath was visited by pillaging bands of both Confederate and Union soldiers. Frequent incursions by the latter forced Joseph Bonner to leave his home in Bath and seek the safety of his plantation at Jackson Swamp. Bonner's son, William Vines Bonner, wrote in 1864 to the Confederate commander, Col. George W. Wortham, stationed at Plymouth. Bonner complained that men under Wortham's command had entered the Bonner House, stolen some clothing, and harassed several of the slaves.[14] The Reverend Israel Harding of St. Thomas Church also fled. The church, left in impoverished circumstances, was unable to compensate the Reverend Luther Eborn, who officiated during the war, although it pledged to do so when possible.[15]

During the Civil War and in the years immediately following, many African Americans departed Bath. Some may have been part of the exodus of more than ten thousand slaves who left plantations in eastern North Carolina to seek a new life. By traveling south fifty miles, they could have established themselves in the large freedman's colony formed outside New Bern at James City in 1863. There, former slaves were provided with houses, employment, and access to schools, churches, and medical care.[16] William Bonner's 1864 letter to Colonel Wortham revealed that his father had "lost already, with a few exceptions, all of his negroes." An elderly man and his wife were two of Bonner's slaves who remained in Bath in the waning days of the war.[17]

During the war, African Americans feared reprisals from both Union and Confederate troops. A case in point was Ned, an enslaved man hired out to Bath resident Rev. H. G. Hilton. In June 1864, Ned was arrested by Confederate troops, who charged him with transporting fugitive slaves to Yankee boats. Several weeks earlier, he had been detained by Union troops, who tried to intimidate him into leaving Bath with the threat of being arrested by Confederate soldiers. Ned chose to remain in Bath and ironically, the forewarning proved true.[18]

Bath after the Civil War

Bath, Beaufort County, and eastern North Carolina recovered slowly after the war. Even though Bath did not witness the fighting and devastation that many nearby towns did, all residents felt the effects on business and everyday life. The Joseph Bonner family found retrenchment mandatory. In February 1868, the Bonner House was occupied by Bonner, his wife Sallie, their daughter Caroline, and their son Thomas and his wife Emily, all of whom lived "upon the most economical plan. We dispensed with our cook a month ago," according to Bonner, since which time, "Emily has done the cooking with good will and cheerfulness. Caroline loaned me money to buy a stove and she has loaned Tom a sufficient sum to buy a barrel of pork. This prevented my family from being broken up." Thomas Bonner, a physician, subsequently left Bath to open a medical practice in Aurora, an indication perhaps of stagnant economic conditions in postwar Bath.[19]

In 1867, polls showed 76 white males and 24 African American males of taxable age, a complete reversal of the ratios before the war.[20] Many former slaves may have left to seek education, to reunify families torn apart by slavery, and often simply to put distance between themselves and their former owners. Perhaps exemplifying slaves who left Bath was David Marsh, who was born on Durham Creek about 1818 and raised in Alabama. By 1870, Marsh was living at James City and employed at cutting crossties. When he opened an account with the Freedmen's Bureau Bank in New Bern that year, he listed his father, also named David Marsh, as residing in Bath.[21] Either or both of the Marshes may have been former slaves of the Marsh family that owned the Palmer-Marsh House during the nineteenth century.

Unlike Marsh, Matilda Simmons was a former Beaufort County slave who chose to remain in the county after the war. Born and raised at Pantego Creek, the fifty-year-old Simmons still claimed that area as her home in 1870. Widowed and living with her twelve-year-old son, Simmons supported her small family by spinning, washing, and cooking. The information that Simmons provided to the Freedmen's Bureau Bank upon opening an account typified the separation of African American families during slavery and Reconstruction. Some of her family lived at Jackson Swamp; her deceased parents had lived on Bath Creek; a half sister lived at James City; and other siblings had been sold and sent out of state.[22]

At the end of the nineteenth century, Bath, a community of 350 to 400 residents, seemed to have revived from the depressing effects of the Civil War. The stimulus for the economic turnaround that the town needed may have come from the bridge that was built across Bath Creek. In July 1887, a site was selected "from the foot of Center Street to Hammock Point on the opposite side" of the creek. The bridge was completed the following spring at a cost to Beaufort County of $3,127.71. Two months later, the *Washington Progress* reported that "the people of Bath seem to be manifesting more interest in the upbuilding of the place since the bridge has been completed. The bridge is a great convenience to the town."[23]

For the next several months, the Washington newspaper mentioned many changes in Bath. In a special edition on October 15, 1889, called *The First Industrial Issue of the Washington Progress*, the paper noted:

> Bath can boast of six well kept stores, a steam mill and to all appearance a fine opening for business men and manufacturing facilities. The health of Bath is good, her people law abiding, courteous and kind and much hospitality and generosity among them. The population has doubled in a few past years can double ten times and there will be room for more good citizens.[24]

The local hotel was remodeled and enlarged the next year. A number of new homes were constructed, and there was a new doctor, several general mercantile firms, and a livery business.

Underpinning the prosperity of the times was the boom in lumber milling in eastern North Carolina, a movement in which Bath participated. Soon after the incorporation of the Bath Manufacturing Company in 1889, the company was milling fifteen thousand board feet of lumber per day. The following year the Roanoke Lumber Company rebuilt an old mill in the vicinity of Bath, and it was rumored that the locally well known Roper Lumber Company was interested in acquiring land in the area. Capt. Cicero H. Brooks moved to Bath from Hyde County and began a sawmill operation on Bath Creek. After his death in 1901, his son Timothy A. Brooks continued and expanded the business. Mill workers brightened the prospects of local businesses and created a demand for rental housing.[25] Several of the structures the younger Brooks built along North Main and Carteret Streets to house workers still serve as residences today. Brooks was a prominent figure in Bath, both in business and civic affairs, well into the twentieth century.

But, as always, the omnipresent water was the cornerstone for the economy of the area. In 1889, the waterways around Bath contained "every variety of fish" and "large moneys have been made . . . conducting the industry of fish catching and shipping."[26] In the late nineteenth century, Joseph Y. Bonner, son of Joseph, owned a small warehouse at Bonner's Point where fish were unloaded and sold to area residents or packed on ice for shipment to Washington and other towns.[27]

Economic activity carried over into the social life of Bath. In 1889 the town reportedly contained one of the best academies in Beaufort County, taught by the rector of St. Thomas Church. The two churches in town, Episcopal and Methodist, were augmented by the appearance of the African Methodist Episcopal (AME) Zion Church about 1897, and by the Christian Church, Disciples of Christ, in 1909. The AME Zion Church, still in use in the 1930s, had been abandoned by 1940, and the building was demolished sometime between 1955 and 1958.[28] Although there were plans to develop the former church lot as part of the restoration of Bath, local residents helped thwart those plans in 1961 by submitting the names of forty-two individuals buried in the cemetery there. A granite marker commemorating the deceased was purchased by the Metropolitan AME Zion Church in Washington and dedicated at Bath during a 1996 ceremony. In 1997, an archaeological exploration of the site located the brick piers upon which the church had been built.[29] The Bath Christian Church organized in 1905, occupied its new sanctuary in 1909, and at this writing enjoys an active congregation. Bath also proved a popular

Students at Bath High School, late 1920s. Photo courtesy of Peggy Kilby Davis, Bath, N.C.

Swindell's Cash Store, formerly the T. A. Brooks Grocery on South Main Street. The store was built in 1905 and closed in 1984 when owner Jack Swindell hung an "Out to Lunch" sign on the door and never returned.

site for religious groups, particularly from Washington, to visit and picnic. A temperance organization, telephone line, and baseball team in the 1890s attested to Bath's successful attempt to stay in the mainstream of American life.[30]

The centennial of Bath's founding may well have passed unrecognized in 1805. A century later, however, Washington resident Lida T. Rodman decided that the two hundredth anniversary should not go unnoticed. She put together the "Souvenir Calendar Ye Old Bath Town 1705-1905." The commemorative calendar contained photographs and drawings of Bath, and historical information about the town and some of its early residents.

Darker Days for Bath

While recent growth and improvement seemed to auger well as Bath entered its third century, several unfortunate occurrences in the early years of the twentieth century once again meant the small town had to recover and rebuild.

On May 19, 1905, the grist and lathe mill located on Bath Creek near Bonner's Point caught fire and in a short time was completely destroyed. The town's only fire protection was a bucket brigade, which was highly praised by the local press for keeping damage to adjacent properties at a minimum. Losses sustained by the Elliott Brothers, owners of the mill, were estimated at $1,800. Damages to the houses across the street, the Thomas B. Clayton and the B. F. Hamilton homes, were valued at $50 and $25, respectively.

This was but the first of several fires to plague the business area of Bath, which ran south along Main Street from the corner of Carteret Street, where the stores, built of wood, were placed close together. The Sunday, April 7, 1918, fire damaged almost an entire block in the business section on South Main Street. It was described by the *Washington Daily News* as the "worst fire which that city has ever experienced," with damages estimated at nearly $15,000. The fire started in the woodstove of the store owned by Capt. Carlton Archbell and destroyed that building as well as the home and store of minister W. O. Winfield. Dr. Nicholson's drugstore, Richard Tarkington's meat market, William W. Mason's store, William H. Duke's garage, and a row of buildings owned by Charles W. Bowen that included the post office incurred additional damage. Timothy A. Brooks's store, built of brick in 1905, was only slightly damaged.

Another fire in 1928 proved even more devastating than earlier conflagrations since it affected buildings on both sides of Main Street. The blaze was first spotted in the rear of the Marsh Store about midnight on October 24 as Mrs. Edgar Tankard, Mrs. James Tyer, and Mrs. William Arnold returned home from the Beaufort County Fair in Washington. The fire may have started on the second floor of the Marsh building, used by the Junior Order United American Mechanics and the Modern Woodmen of the World. The flames quickly spread through the entire building. The first floor housed the Marsh drugstore and Thad Tankard's barbershop. Wind was a factor in this fire, sending sparks across Main Street and causing the destruction of the home of Mrs. Tankard, a barn belonging to Marsh, and the Draper building, where about seventeen thousand pounds of tobacco were stored. Once again, the bucket brigade sprang into action. In addition, Washington sent a pumping engine that used water from the creek to help prevent the fire from spreading. Damage was estimated at between $25,000 and $35,000, only a small portion of which was covered by insurance.

While these fires were setbacks for the town and its businessmen, the most tragic event of the twentieth century was the drowning of four people on the gas boat *Marion*. Although the bridge was an asset to the town and its commerce, much travel was still done by water, since few people had motor vehicles. Many of the crops grown locally for export, including potatoes, were also sent out by boat. Often those vessels accepted passengers.

Thomas Draper's photograph of the heavily laden *Marion*, which sank in 1916 with the loss of four passengers.

On the morning of June 16, 1916, the *Marion* was on a routine run to Washington, loaded with potatoes. Several men from the area, as well as three teenaged girls, were along for the ride. Maud Mason, age fourteen, was on her way for a piano lesson; and Ruth Brooks, age fourteen, and her sister Katie, age eighteen, were going to pick out the older girl's wedding dress. When the *Marion* left Bath, several people on shore noted that it appeared as though it was not loaded properly. The boat first stopped at Archbell Point to pick up more potatoes from J. B. Archbell's farm. Bath resident and businessman G. W. Marsh got off the boat there because he believed it was overloaded and that going any farther was a great risk. It turned out that he made a wise decision. Just off the point, the boat made the turn for Washington, and the weight of the load, possibly paired with a swell, caused the boat to overturn and sink. The three girls were in the pilothouse, and all attempts to rescue them failed. Their bodies were recovered and brought to the wharf at Bath, where further attempts to revive them were unsuccessful. The fourth victim was passenger J. S. Woolard, age sixty-one, whose body was found later that day.

Coincidentally, Bath photographer Thomas R. Draper captured on film the fully loaded *Marion* riding low in the water sometime before her sinking. Draper set up business in Bath in 1890 and lived there until his death in 1940. From a small souvenir shop on Main Street he sold postcards made from his photographs.

Draper's work offers rare views of Bath commercial life, street scenes, and people in the early twentieth century.

During the first quarter of the twentieth century, the North Carolina legislature twice enlarged the boundaries of Bath, but not as a result of an increasing population, as the number of residents declined from 400 in 1900 to 274 in 1920. A mayor and a commission of three governed the town. In 1921, an all-female commission successfully campaigned for a paved road to connect Bath to Washington and for a marker to commemorate the original incorporation of Bath. The next year witnessed the completion of Bath High School. Lumbering and fishing continued to dominate the economy.[31]

Thomas R. Draper, photographer of early-nineteenth-century Bath.

Bath after a rare snowstorm, ca. 1930, looking northward along South Main Street. Photograph by Thomas R. Draper.

The Bath Monument

Bath's historical importance to North Carolina was illuminated soon after the production of the two-hundredth-anniversary calendar. A nascent historical preservation movement led to the formation of the Bath Historical Society in the early twentieth century. The group met monthly for several years with the goal of bringing history to the forefront through active participation. Several members of the community, as well as some state and county historians, felt that the incorporation and history of Bath deserved recognition. To that end, the North Carolina Historical Commission and the Beaufort County Board of Commissioners in September 1918 presented the historical society with a bronze plaque commemorating the founding and incorporation of Bath. Although plans were apparently in place to mount the plaque on the wall of St. Thomas Church, for unknown reasons the installation never occurred.[32]

Thus arose the need for a monument on which to display the plaque. Mr. and Mrs. Timothy A. Brooks and Miss Lida T. Rodman traveled to the Neverson Quarry near Raleigh to select stones for the marker. Two pieces were chosen by the group and donated to Bath. The base weighed sixteen thousand pounds and the top twelve thousand pounds. The stones were shipped by Norfolk-Southern Railroad to Bunyan, about ten miles west of Bath. Brooks sent a truck and trailer to Bunyan to bring the stones to Bath, but because the road from Washington to Bath was unpaved, the bumpy ride caused both pieces to roll out of the truck and settle into the mire on the side of the road. A call for help went out to Surry Bowen in Pinetown, who sent equipment to reload the boulders. The next hurdle was the bridge at Bath Creek. It was uncertain whether the wooden structure could handle a load of this tonnage. Brooks again offered his services, using heavy wooden beams from his mill to brace the bridge. Finally arriving and taking its place at the intersection of Main and Carteret Streets, the marker was installed and the plaque affixed to the front.

A huge celebration was planned to unveil the marker on June 19, 1924. People from all over the county assisted. Thirty-two pigs were donated for the meal, and men cooked all night to have barbecue ready for the expected crowds. Schoolchildren were enlisted and by means of a contest raised the money needed to purchase the remainder of the food items on the menu. The student who brought in the most money would have the honor of unveiling the marker. Helen Waters and Mary Arcadia Tankard, who tied for first place, shared the privilege. Altogether the children raised $150, of which only $50 was needed for food. The remaining money surplus was donated to the Bath Elementary School library for books and, along with bookcases built by Marion Brooks, brought the library up to state accreditation standards.

Draper photograph of Mary Arcadia Tankard (*left*) and Helen Waters (*right*) on the marker commemorating the founding of Bath, dedicated in 1924.

An estimated four thousand people attended the celebration and heard the address by former congressman Lindsay C. Warren. He closed his speech by saying, "May it [the tablet and marker] keep alive the memory of a sturdy race who crossed trackless seas, who blazed the wilderness, who endured hardships and privations and who built a civilization. They succeeded because back of their hard exteriors there was force, determination and character."[33] The marker was moved from its original location to North Main Street in 1960 when the present bridge across Bath Creek was built and Carteret Street widened to allow for the paving of Highway 92 through Bath.

The marker was erected in time for the large number of visitors who descended upon Bath in 1925. Most of them were Episcopalians from across the state that had begun to view a trip to St. Thomas as a sort of pilgrimage. Those treks, which often involved as many as three hundred people and included the celebration of Holy Communion, were especially memorable as the colonial church could only seat a little more than one hundred. The pilgrimages continued for several years and were probably the most important impetus that led to the restoration of the historic church. The congregation was small and financially unable to correct the structural deterioration that afflicted the ancient sanctuary.

Bishop Thomas Darst, who had taken a special interest in restoring the church, led the services in 1925. Soon thereafter, "The Association for the Restoration and Preservation of St. Thomas Episcopal Church, Bath" was born. The goal of this group was to restore the church in time for its two hundredth anniversary in 1934. Actual work on the building was minimal because of a lack of funds, so by 1934 very little progress could be seen. Bishop Darst realized that in order to accomplish the restoration, someone had to take control at the local level. His search for a rector who shared his vision for St. Thomas was answered in 1936 with the arrival of the Reverend Alexander Constantine Davis Noe.

The Reverend Mr. Noe began his work by forming a new action group, the Bath Restoration Committee. The committee would also be concerned with improving some of the other historical structures in town, but St. Thomas was the first priority. Noe recruited the help of local workmen, and by the fall of 1939 the group had successfully straightened the bulging walls, reinforced the foundation with concrete, and put on a new shingle roof on the old church.

With the successful completion of what many had thought impossible, the group was energized. Soon the once neglected small church looked as though it had been under constant care. Many of the changes of a Victorian nature that had been made in the late nineteenth century were removed, and through research the structure reassumed the appearance of a colonial place of worship, but with electricity. Among the alterations removed were a bead board ceiling, Queen Anne-style windows, and ornate oil lamps that had probably been installed in the 1880s. The floor tiles, once set only in sand, were permanently installed in cement. Only a few of the original tiles remained by that time as tourists had removed them for souvenirs over the years. The remaining tiles, now worn but once decorated with dragonheads and flowers, were placed in the chancel, and new tiles were purchased to finish the floor.

The Reverend Alexander Constantine Davis Noe, who led the effort to restore St. Thomas Episcopal Church in the late 1930s.

By the end of the Reverend Mr. Noe's first five years at St. Thomas, the goal of saving the church as a historic structure had finally been achieved. Once the appearance of the church was improved, attention turned to the beautification of the grounds. Noe was very interested in an earlier proposal for the building of a ballast rock wall to encompass the church grounds. Much of the waterfront was littered with those rocks, which had been used on ships as weight, and thus reflected the shipping and commercial history of the town. Youth, as well as adults, in the town spent hours retrieving ballast rocks from the mud and silt

The interior of the restored St. Thomas Episcopal Church, 1946.

close to shore. Within two years, they had created a huge mountain on the church property. Often their pay came directly from the rector's own pocket. Sadly, the wall that now surrounds the churchyard was not erected until 1979, the year after his death.

With the church structure stabilized, the Reverend Mr. Noe's focus turned to rekindling the spirit of worship as well as increasing his congregation's cognizance of their church's unique place in history. This awareness spread not only throughout the state but also well beyond. A special service held on the second Sunday in June 1944 quickly became a tradition. Bride and Groom Day was devoted to couples who were married at St. Thomas to return and renew their vows. The procession, led by the pair married the longest and ending with the most recently wedded, entered the church to traditional wedding music. The rector's favorite blessing for these couples was, "May your sweethearts be your wives and your wives always be your sweethearts." Even after his retirement in 1953, Noe continued to participate in this ritual as long as his health allowed. These services were followed by a picnic dinner on the grounds.

Reverend A. C. D. Noe died on December 7, 1978, at the age of ninety-eight and was buried in the St. Thomas Church cemetery. Even though he was rector of the church for only seventeen years, he served the parish more than forty-two years. A plaque to his memory was placed in the church. It honors his vision for St. Thomas, noting that he was instrumental in the "preservation of this sacred place of worship from ruin in the 1930s and served as inspiration and impetus for the general restoration of Bath historic treasures."

Edna Ferber and *Show Boat*

The most celebrated visitor to Bath in the memorable year of 1925 was Edna Ferber, author of *Cimarron*, *Giant*, and the Pulitzer Prize winner, *So Big*. Deemed perhaps the greatest female novelist of her time, Ferber went to Bath to see the *James Adams Floating Theatre* in order to gather material for her forthcoming novel, *Show Boat*. She found Bath "a lovely decayed hamlet . . . [whose] ancient houses, built by men who knew dignity of architectural design and purity of line, were now mouldering into the dust from which they came."[34] The *James Adams Floating Theatre*, which wintered in Elizabeth City, made Bath its first stop in the 1925 season. Ferber spent three days in Henry Ormond's boardinghouse (the Palmer-Marsh House) while waiting to board the vessel. Her stay on the floating theatre greatly influenced the writing of *Show Boat*, in which there is a direct reference to "Bath, on the Pamlico River."[35] This novel inspired a long-running Broadway musical and two movie versions.

Edna Ferber, who visited Bath in 1925 to gather material for an upcoming novel.

The *James Adams Floating Theatre* was a regular visitor to Bath between 1914 and the late 1930s. The 128-foot long and 34-foot wide vessel contained a theatre that seated over five hundred and accommodations for thirty-two personnel traveling with the show. The "Show Boat,"[36] as it was called, was built in Washington at the Farrow Shipyard in 1913. It was one of the last of the showboats to travel the waterways of the United States.

Bath's 250th Anniversary Celebration — October 1-4, 1955

The ensuing decades passed quietly in Bath. The country was in the grips of the Great Depression, and few improvements were made in the infrastructure of the town. New construction was rare. But the absence of affluence did not stop the citizens of Bath and Beaufort County from recognizing Bath's 250th anniversary. For four days in early October 1955, the town held a grand celebration to mark the anniversary of its incorporation and its status as the oldest town in North Carolina. Plans and preparations for the occasion were briefly disrupted by three hurricanes— Connie (August 12), Diane (August 17), and Ione (September 19)—that tore through the area in the two months prior to the festivities. Bath's citizens rallied behind the clean-up effort, and the town was ready to host the more than five thousand visitors who flocked to the anniversary events.

The celebration was designed for wide appeal with a focus on both history and entertainment. A history of colonial Bath was written by Herbert Paschal and published in time to be sold during the October events. A large plaster birthday cake with electric candles formed a focal point in the center of the business district along South Main Street. More than three hundred of the town's male residents grew beards, moustaches, goatees, or sideburns in an effort to appear historically accurate in their colonial costumes. So great was the pressure to conform to this endeavor that fake moustaches were available for those who didn't want to be hirsute Judging of the "Brothers of the Brush" was included as part of the pirate celebration and street dance. Silver cups donated by area jewelry stores were awarded to the five winners.

"Brothers of the Brush," winners of silver cups for the best beards at the 250th anniversary of the founding of Bath in 1955.

The maritime history of Bath and the town's connection to Blackbeard and piracy were not forgotten. Pirates debarked from a masted ship that had sailed into Bath Creek from the Pamlico River and invaded the town. Tossing handfuls of "gold" coins and bejeweled necklaces, the pirates fired muskets and chased women and children through the streets. A street dance was moved to the school gymnasium when rain interrupted the occasion.

St. Thomas Episcopal Church celebrated with a colonial service its status as the state's oldest standing church. The Bath Methodist and Christian churches also held homecoming services that weekend. Mr. and Mrs. William B. Midgette and their granddaughter, Miss Diane Petway, hosted a barbecue reception for North Carolina governor Luther H. Hodges, who was in town for many of the events. Three hundred guests attended the gala celebration, which was held at Kirby Grange, site of Christopher Gale's home. The governor and his wife were also entertained with a formal tea at the Glebe House and an outdoor concert by the Cherry Point Air Wing Band.

Culminating the celebration was the performance of an outdoor play, *Queen Anne's Bell*. Written and narrated by Edmund Hoyt Harding, the play featured music, dancing, and fourteen scenes of events significant to Bath's history. Governor and Mrs. Hodges, author Inglis Fletcher, Attorney General William B. Rodman, and Lindsay C. Warren performed in starring roles to the standing-room-only audience. Many of Bath's schoolchildren were also among the cast of more than three hundred. *The Lost Colony,* the long-running outdoor drama on Roanoke Island, loaned lighting for the play. The celebration was a resounding success. The total cost was $17,039, of which the State of North Carolina provided $2,500; the other funds came from private and business donations and from ticket sales for the drama and other events.

The town's celebration and recognition of Bath's importance to the history of the state probably helped promote the

Governor Luther Hodges in costume for his starring role in *Queen Anne's Ball.*

preservation movement in Bath. The "ancient houses" to which Edna Ferber referred during her 1925 visit attracted intense interest during the 250th observance. The renewed awareness of Bath's history resulted in the creation of the Beaufort County Historical Society, the Historic Bath Commission, and the

Historic Bath State Historic Site. St. Thomas Church, owned by the Diocese of East Carolina, had already undergone extensive restoration work in the previous decade and a half under the leadership of the Reverend Noe The Beaufort County Historical Society, organized in 1955 under the leadership of Edmund Hoyt Harding of Washington, began a fund-raising drive in 1957 to acquire and restore the Palmer-Marsh House and the Bonner House. As a result, the historical society, aided by the active efforts of newspaperman and public official Capus Waynick, was able to obtain the Palmer-Marsh House from the Ormond family in 1958.[37]

Recognizing the work of the historical society, the General Assembly in 1959 created the Historic Bath Commission "for the Purpose of the Acquisition, Repair and Maintenance of Historic Sites in the Town of Bath in Beaufort County." With Edmund H. Harding as its chair, the Historic Bath Commission first met in January 1960 and began restoration of the Palmer-Marsh House. Once this project was well under way, the commission secured a grant from the Oscar F. Smith Memorial Foundation that enabled the Beaufort County Historical Society to buy, restore, and furnish the Bonner House. The historical society later purchased the AME Zion Church (cemetery) lot and additional land behind the Bonner House. In May 1962 it opened the furnished Palmer-Marsh and Bonner Houses to the public.[38] Volunteer guides in period dress provided tours of both houses.

Washington native Edmund H. Harding was the driving force behind the restoration of Bath. A former insurance and fertilizer salesman turned public speaker, Harding used his considerable charm and boundless energy to great advantage. In his roles as president of the Beaufort County Historical Society

and chairman of the Historic Bath Commission, Harding was instrumental in the acquisition and restoration of the Palmer-Marsh and Bonner Houses. In commemoration of his tireless efforts in Bath, Harding was made honorary mayor for life and Carteret Street was renamed in his honor.[39]

Despite the remarkable success of the Beaufort County Historical Society and the Historic Bath Commission, the need

Edmund Hoyt Harding of Washington, leader of the movement for the restoration and preservation of Bath in the mid-twentieth century.

for additional funding and personnel to interpret, maintain, and continue the restoration of properties in Bath convinced the General Assembly in 1963 to designate Historic Bath as a state historic site, administered by what is now the Office of Archives and History, North Carolina Department of Cultural Resources. Thus Historic Bath became part of the burgeoning state historic sites program that had been inaugurated in 1955. The Beaufort County Historical Society transferred the Palmer-Marsh House, the Bonner House and associated properties, and the AME Zion Church lot to the state in 1964. The Van Der Veer House, donated to the Beaufort County Historical Society in 1968 by Ruth Bowen Smith, was deeded by the society to the state in 1970, and moved from its original location to its present position on the grounds of the state historic site.[40] It opened in 1987, with exhibit space on the history of the town. The state built a visitor center in 1970 featuring an orientation film.

Historic Bath State Historic Site continues to be a popular visitor destination. Visitation reached record levels in the mid-1980s, during the production of an outdoor drama, *Blackbeard: Knight of the Black Flag*. Held along the waterfront on North Main Street at the edge of what is now the Catnip Point development, the play, written by Stuart Aronson, was performed from 1977 to 1986. The play centered on Blackbeard and his time in Bath and included fact as well as legend. Local residents comprised a large portion of the cast.

A devastating fire struck the Palmer-Marsh House in the early morning hours of December 10, 1989. Within minutes of the fire's discovery by a local resident, the fire department was battling the blaze and townspeople were helping site staff to save the building's furnishings. It was later determined that an electrical problem was the cause of the fire. The house officially reopened to the public in December 1993, after a painstaking restoration that included analysis of the original interior and exterior paint colors. The tragedy also afforded researchers the opportunity to perform tree-ring dating, or dendrochronology, on the structural timbers of the house. This analysis determined that the house was originally constructed around 1751.

Thus the heritage of eighteenth-century Bath, North Carolina's first incorporated town, has been well preserved. The maritime activity of the former port can now only be imagined. Yet several significant structures—St. Thomas Church, cared for by the Diocese of East Carolina; and the Palmer-Marsh House, the Bonner House, and the Van Der Veer House, preserved through the efforts of the Beaufort County Historical Society and the Historic Bath Commission, and now managed as a state historic site—remain as tangible evidence of life in early Bath. Further, the town, whose appearance in 1705 antedated the settlement of most of present North Carolina, stands as a reminder of the longevity and enduring richness of the state's history.

NOTES

1. Clark, *State Records*, 24:764-765; Powell, *North Carolina Gazetteer*, 518; Reed, *Beaufort County*, 102-109.

2. Paschal, *History of Colonial Bath*, 42.

3. Saunders, *Colonial Records*, 10:717; Clark, *State Records*, 11:355, 490, 601, 645; 13:189; 15:337; 22:750.

4. Donald Jackson and Dorothy Twohig, eds., *The Diaries of George Washington*, 6 vols. (Charlottesville, Va.: University Press of Virginia, 1976-1979), 6:112-115; Clark, *State Records*, 16:736-737; Angley, "Bonner House Vicinity of Bath," 118; Angley, "Port Bath," 5-6; 1st Cong., 2d sess., c. 1, *The Public Statutes at Large of the United States of America, from the Organization of the Government in 1789, to March 3, 1845*. 8 vols. (Boston: Charles C. Little and James Brown, 1845-1867), 1:99-101; William Latham, "Hydrographic Map of Virginia and North Carolina," 1807; R. H. B. Brazier, "Swamplands Between Albemarle and Pamplico Sounds," 1828.

5. Cross, "Palmer-Marsh House"; Jerry L. Cross, "Historical Research Report, Van Der Veer House, Bath, North Carolina" (report, Research Branch, Division of Archives and History, Raleigh, October 1975), 4-6; Angley, "Bonner House Vicinity of Bath," 48.

6. Catherine W. Bishir and Michael T. Southern, *A Guide to the Historic Architecture of Eastern North Carolina* (Chapel Hill: University of North Carolina Press, 1996), 181; Angley, "Bonner House Vicinity of Bath," 48-60.

7. Angley, "Bonner House Vicinity of Bath," 69; Angley, "History of St. Thomas Episcopal Church," 91-98, 103.

8. Angley, "History of St. Thomas Episcopal Church," 98-99; *Washington Gazette*, November 12, 1891; *Washington Progress*, June 19, 1894; Nancy Chalker, comp., "The History of Bath United Methodist Church, 1892-1992," (ca. 1992).

9. McCartney, "History [of] Bath Town."

10. Beaufort County, Abstract of Taxes, 1832-1852, State Archives, Office of Archives and History, Raleigh.

11. *Heads of Families at the First Census of the United States Taken in the Year 1790: North Carolina* (Washington: Government Printing Office, 1908), 10.

12. Carter G. Woodson, ed., *Free Negro Owners of Slaves in the United States in 1830* (Washington: Association for the Study of Negro Life and History, 1924), 24.

13. *North State Whig* (Washington, N.C.), August 14, December 4, 1850; January 29, February 19, March 26, May 21, 1851; Wesley H. Wallace, "North Carolina's Agricultural Journals, 1838-1861," *North Carolina Historical Review* 36 (July 1959): 280; Angley, "Bonner House Vicinity of Bath," 72.

14. William Bonner to Col. George W. Wortham, June 16, 1864, Thomas M. Pittman Papers, Private Collections, State Archives, Office of Archives and History, Raleigh.

15. Angley, "Bonner House Vicinity of Bath," 88; Angley, "History of St. Thomas Episcopal Church," 103-105.

16. Joe A. Mobley, *James City: A Black Community in North Carolina, 1863-1900* (Raleigh: Division of Archives and History, Department of Cultural Resources, 1981), 25.

17. Bonner to Wortham, June 16, 1864, Pittman Papers.

18. H. G. Hilton to Col. George W. Wortham, June 18, 1864, Pittman Papers.

19. Angley, "Bonner House Vicinity of Bath," 89-91, 97.

20. Beaufort County, Abstract of Taxes.

21. Bill Reaves, *North Carolina Freedman's Savings and Trust Company Records* (Raleigh: North Carolina Genealogical Society, 1992), 185.

22. Reaves, *North Carolina Freedman's Records*, 41.

23. *Washington Weekly Progress*, July 12, 1887; *Washington Progress*, April 10, June 5, 1888.

24. *The First Industrial Issue of the Washington Progress*, October 15, 1889.

25. *Washington Progress*, January 31, 1888; October 15, 1889; *Washington Gazette*, October 24, 1889; *Bath Budget*, February 20, June 19, December 18, 1890; Angley, "Bonner House Vicinity of Bath," 106-107.

26. *Washington Gazette*, November 1, 1889.

27. Angley, "Bonner House Vicinity of Bath," 105.

28. Mrs. Cottie Boyd, oral interview, August 21, 2003. Tape recording on file at Historic Bath State Historic Site, Bath, N.C.

29. Steven Allen, *Archaeological Investigations at the Bath African Methodist Episcopal Church Site* (Bath, N.C.: Division of Archives and History, Historic Sites Section, 1998).

30. Stanley L. Little,"Bath African Methodist Episcopal Zion Church" (report, Division of State Historic Sites, Raleigh, 2003); "History of the Bath Christian Church" (n.d.); *Washington Progress*, March 7, August 7, 1888; May 22, 1894; January 5, February 24, 1897; *Washington Gazette*, November 1, 1889; February 7, 1895; *Bath Budget*, February 20, May 15, 1890.

31. Michelle F. Lawing, "Historical Research Report on Edna Ferber's Visit to Bath, North Carolina" (report, Research Branch, Division of Archives and History, Raleigh, June 1979), 8-9; *News and Observer* (Raleigh), March 26, 1921; "Bath High School[;] Bath Elementary School[;] Timeline," (n.d.).

32. *Seventh Biennial Report of the North Carolina Historical Commission* (Raleigh: Edwards and Broughton Printing Company, 1919), 17.

33. "Address of the Honorable Lindsay C. Warren delivered at Bath, June 19th[,] 1924[,] on the occasion of the unveiling of the tablet erected by the State Historical Commission to commemorate the 219th anniversary of the incorporation of the town," unpublished speech, copies on file, Historic Bath State Historic Site, Bath, N.C.

34. Edna Ferber, *A Peculiar Treasure* (New York: Doubleday, Duran and Company, 1939), 296.

35. Angley, "History of St. Thomas Episcopal Church," 128-130; Lawing, "Edna Ferber's Visit," 10-13, 25-26.

36. Ursula F. Loy and Pauline M. Worthy, eds., *Washington and the Pamlico* (Raleigh: Edwards and Broughton Company, 1976), 141.

37. Angley, "History of St. Thomas Episcopal Church," 135-137; Angley, "Bonner House Vicinity of Bath," 121-122; Cross, "Palmer-Marsh House"; Correspondence, 1958, Capus Miller Waynick Papers, East Carolina Manuscript Collection, East Carolina University, Greenville.

38. *Session Laws of North Carolina, 1959,* c. 1005; Angley, "Bonner House Vicinity of Bath," 121-132. Other goals proposed in 1959 by the Historic Bath Commission, including the preservation of the Buzzard Hotel, the construction of a Native American village, and the development of Plum Point,

were not to be realized. Wilson Angley, "The Life and Work of Edmund H. Harding," (report, Research Branch, Division of Archives and History, Raleigh, 1980), 30.

39. Loy and Worthy, *Washington and the Pamlico*, 495.

40. *Session Laws of North Carolina, 1963*, c. 997; Cross, "Palmer-Marsh House"; Cross, "Van Der Veer House," 7; Angley, "Bonner House Vicinity of Bath," 132-133; Gerald W. Butler, manager, Historic Bath State Historic Site, letters to author, March 14, 22, 2001. For the history of the state historic sites, see Robert R. Garvey Jr., "North Carolina's State Historic Sites," in *Public History in North Carolina, 1903-1978*, ed. Jeffrey J. Crow (Raleigh: Division of Archives and History, Department of Cultural Resources, 1979), 54-64.

Bibliography

Primary Sources

Government and Official Records

Library of Congress, Washington, D.C.
   "An Account of Duties Collected and the Fines and Forfeitures recovered in the several ports now under the American Commission, Oct. 10, 1766 and Oct. 10, 1767." Treasury Papers, 1/452, f. 47. Photostat.

North Carolina State Archives, Office of Archives and History, Raleigh, N.C.

Beaufort County, Abstract of Taxes, 1832-1852.

Beaufort County, Minutes of the Beaufort County Court of Pleas and Quarter Sessions.

Beaufort County, Record of Deeds.

Beaufort County Tax List, 1755, Treasurer's and Comptroller's Papers.

R. H. B. Brazier Map. "Swamplands Between Albemarle and Pamplico Sounds." 1828.

Colonial Court Records, General Court, Criminal Papers, 1730-1734.

William Latham Map. "Hydrographic Map of Virginia and North Carolina." 1807.

"The Memorial of Robert Palmer[,] Surveyor Gen[era]l of the Lands in No[rth] Carol[ina,] One of His Majesty's Council and late Collector of the port of Bath Town." December 30, 1783. Audit Office, 12/36. Microfilm.

Henry Mouzon Map. 1775.

C. J. Sauthier Maps of Bath, Edenton, and New Bern. 1769.

Secretary of State Papers, Magistrates and Freeholders Courts, 1715-1793.

Southern Historical Collection, University of North Carolina, Chapel Hill, N.C.

Ledger of Imports and Exports, British North American Ports, 1768-1773. Customs, 16/1. Photocopies.

Manuscript Collections

North Carolina State Archives, Office of Archives and History, Raleigh, N.C.

Thomas M. Pittman Papers.

East Carolina Manuscript Collection, East Carolina University, Greenville, N.C.

Capus Miller Waynick Papers.

Newspapers

Bath Budget.

News and Observer (Raleigh).

North State Whig (Washington, N.C.).

South Carolina Gazette (Charleston).

Virginia Gazette (Williamsburg).

Washington (N.C.) *Gazette.*

Washington (N.C.) *Progress.*

Washington (N.C.) *Weekly Progress.*

Printed Documentary Sources

Barnwell, Joseph W., ed. "The Second Tuscarora Expedition." *South Carolina Magazine of History and Biography* 10 (January 1909): 33-48.

Brickell, John. *The Natural History of North Carolina.* Murfreesboro, N.C.: Johnson Publishing Company, 1968, orig. 1737.

Clark, Walter, ed. *The State Records of North Carolina.* 16 vols., numbered 11-26. Raleigh: State of North Carolina, 1895-1906.

Corbitt, David Leroy, ed. *Explorations, Descriptions, and Attempted Settlements of Carolina, 1584-1590.* Rev. ed. Raleigh: State Department of Archives and History, 1953.

Finlay, Hugh. *Journal Kept by Hugh Finlay, Surveyor of the Post Roads on the Continent of North America.* Brooklyn: Frank H. Norton, 1867.

Grimes, J. Bryan, ed. *North Carolina Wills and Inventories.* Raleigh: Edwards and Broughton Printing Company, 1912.

Heads of Families at the First Census of the United States Taken in the Year 1790: North Carolina. (Washington: Government Printing Office, 1908).

Jackson, Donald, and Dorothy Twohig, eds. *The Diaries of George Washington*. 6 vols. Charlottesville: University Press of Virginia, 1976-1979.

Johnston, Hugh Buckner, ed. "The Journal of Ebenezer Hazard in North Carolina, 1777 and 1778." *North Carolina Historical Review* 36 (July 1959): 358-381.

"Journal of a French Traveller in the Colonies, I." *American Historical Review* 26 (July 1921): 726-747.

"Journal of Josiah Quincy, Junior, 1773." Massachusetts Historical Society *Proceedings* 49 (1916): 424-481.

Lawson, John. *A New Voyage to Carolina*. Ed. Hugh T. Lefler. Chapel Hill: University of North Carolina Press, 1967.

Lennon, Donald R., and Ida B. Kellam, eds. *The Wilmington Town Book, 1743-1778*. Raleigh: Division of Archives and History, Department of Cultural Resources, 1973.

"William Logan's Journal of a Journey to Georgia, 1745." *Pennsylvania Magazine of History and Biography* 36 (1912): 1-16.

Loy, Ursula F., and Pauline M. Worthy, eds. *Washington and the Pamlico*. Raleigh: Edwards and Broughton Company, 1976.

Parker, Mattie Erma Edwards, et al., eds. *The Colonial Records of North Carolina [Second Series]*. 10 vols. to date. Raleigh: Division of Archives and History, Department of Cultural Resources, 1963-1999.

Phillips, Catherine. *Memories of the Life of Catherine Phillips: To Which Are Added Some of Her Epistles*. Philadelphia: Budd and Bartram, 1797.

The Public Statutes at Large of the United States of America, from the Organization of the Government in 1789, to March 3, 1845. 8 vols. Boston: Charles C. Little and James Brown, 1845-1867.

Reaves, Bill. *North Carolina Freedman's Savings and Trust Company Records*. Raleigh: North Carolina Genealogical Society, 1992.

Saunders, William L., ed. *The Colonial Records of North Carolina*. 10 vols. Raleigh: State of North Carolina, 1886-1890.

Schaw, Janet. *Journal of a Lady of Quality*. Ed. Evangeline Walker Andrews and Charles McLean Andrews. New Haven: Yale University Press, 1923.

Schoepf, Johann David. *Travels in the Confederation, 1783-1784*. Trans. and ed. Alfred J. Morrison. 2 vols. Philadelphia: William J. Campbell, 1911.

Session Laws of North Carolina, 1959, c. 1005; *1963*, c. 997.

Smyth, John Ferdinand Dalziel. *A Tour in the United States of America*. 2 vols. New York: Arno Press, 1968, orig. 1784.

"The Tuscarora Expedition. Letters of Colonel John Barnwell." *South Carolina Magazine of History and Biography* 9 (January 1908): 28-54.

Watson, Elkanah. *Men and Times of the Revolution; or Memoirs of Elkanah Watson*. Ed. Winslow C. Watson. New York: Dana and Company, 1856.

Whitefield, George. *George Whitefield's Journals (1737-1741)*. Gainesville, Fla.: Scholars' Facsimiles and Reprints, 1969.

Secondary Sources

Books and Articles

Allen, Steven. *Archaeological Investigations at the Bath African Methodist Episcopal Church Site*. Bath, N.C.: Division of Archives and History, Historic Sites Section, 1998.

Barrow, Thomas C. *Trade and Empire in Colonial America: The British Customs Service, 1660-1775*. Cambridge, Mass.: Harvard University Press, 1967.

Bishir, Catherine W. *North Carolina Architecture*. Chapel Hill: University of North Carolina Press, 1990.

_____, Charlotte V. Brown, Carl R. Lounsbury, and Ernest H. Wood III. *Architects and Builders in North Carolina: A History of the Practice of Building*. Chapel Hill: University of North Carolina Press, 1990.

_____, and Michael T. Southern. *A Guide to the Historic Architecture of Eastern North Carolina*. Chapel Hill: University of North Carolina Press, 1996.

Butler, Lindley S. "The Early Settlement of Carolina." *Virginia Magazine of History and Biography* 79 (January 1971): 20-28.

_____. "The Governors of Albemarle County, 1663-1689." *North Carolina Historical Review* 46 (summer 1969): 281-299.

_____. *Pirates, Privateers, and Rebel Raiders of the Carolina Coast*. Chapel Hill: University of North Carolina Press, 2000.

Cecelski, David. *A Historian's Coast: Adventures into the Tidewater Past*. Winston-Salem: John Blair, 2000.

Cheney, John L., Jr., ed. *North Carolina Government: A Narrative and Statistical History, 1585-1979*. Raleigh: North Carolina Department of the Secretary of State, 1981.

Cheshire, Joseph Blount, ed. *Sketches of Church History in North Carolina*. Wilmington, N.C.: William L. DeRosset Jr., 1892.

Corbitt, David Leroy, ed. *The Formation of the North Carolina Counties, 1663-1943*. Raleigh: State Department of Archives and History, 1950.

Crittenden, Charles Christopher. *The Commerce of North Carolina, 1763-1789*. New Haven: Yale University Press, 1936.

_____. "Means of Communication in North Carolina, 1763-1789." *North Carolina Historical Review* 8 (October 1931): 373-383.

Crow, Jeffrey J. *The Black Experience in Revolutionary North Carolina*. Raleigh: Division of Archives and History, Department of Cultural Resources, 1977.

_____, Paul D. Escott, and Flora J. Hatley. *A History of African Americans in North Carolina*. Rev. ed. Raleigh: Office of Archives and History, Department of Cultural Resources, 2002.

Diket, A. L. "The Noble Savage Convention as Epitomized in John Lawson's *A New Voyage to Carolina*." *North Carolina Historical Review* 43 (autumn 1966): 413-429.

Dunbar, Gary S. *Historical Geography of the North Carolina Outer Banks*. Baton Rouge: Louisiana State University Press, 1958.

Durant, David. *Ralegh's Lost Colony*. New York: Atheneum, 1981.

Ekirch, A. Roger. *"Poor Carolina": Politics and Society in Colonial North Carolina, 1729-1776*. Chapel Hill: University of North Carolina Press, 1981.

Fagg, Daniel W., Jr. "Sleeping Not with the King's Grant: A Rereading of Some Proprietary Documents, 1663-1667." *North Carolina Historical Review* 48 (spring 1971): 171-185.

Fairchild, Hoxie Neale. *The Noble Savage: A Study in Romantic Naturalism*. New York: Columbia University Press, 1928.

Ferber, Edna. *A Peculiar Treasure*. New York: Doubleday, Duran and Company, 1939.

Garvey, Robert R., Jr. "North Carolina's State Historic Sites." In *Public History in North Carolina, 1903-1978*. Ed. Jeffrey J. Crow. Raleigh: Division of Archives and History, Department of Cultural Resources, 1979.

Goldenberg, Joseph. "Names and Numbers: Statistical Notes on Some Port Records of Colonial North Carolina." *American Neptune* 29 (1969): 155-166.

Greene, Jack P. *The Quest for Power: The Lower Houses of Assembly in the Southern Royal Colonies, 1689-1776*. Chapel Hill: University of North Carolina Press, 1963.

Hinshaw, Seth B. *The Carolina Quaker Experience, 1665-1985*. Greensboro, N.C.: Friends Historical Society, 1984.

Kopperman, Paul E. "Profile of Failure: The Carolana Project, 1629-1640." *North Carolina Historical Review* 59 (winter 1982): 1-23.

Lee, Lawrence. *The Lower Cape Fear in Colonial Days*. Chapel Hill: University of North Carolina Press, 1965.

Lefler, Hugh T. "Promotional Literature of the Southern Colonies." *Journal of Southern History* 33 (February 1967): 3-25.

_____, and William S. Powell. *Colonial North Carolina: A History*. New York: Charles Scribner's Sons, 1973.

Lemmon, Sarah McCulloh. "The Genesis of the Protestant Episcopal Diocese of North Carolina, 1701-1823." *North Carolina Historical Review* 28 (October 1951): 426-462.

_____. "Nathaniel Blount: Last Clergyman of the 'Old Church.' " *North Carolina Historical Review* 50 (autumn 1973): 351-364.

Lennon, Donald R. "The Development of Town Government in Colonial North Carolina." In *Of Tar Heel Towns, Shipbuilders, Reconstructionists and Alliance Men*. Greenville, N.C.: East Carolina University Publications, Department of History, 1981.

Lewis, Clifford, S. J. Loomie, and Albert J. Loomie. *The Spanish Jesuit Mission in Virginia, 1570-1572*. Chapel Hill: University of North Carolina Press, 1953.

London, Lawrence F. "The Representation Controversy in North Carolina." *North Carolina Historical Review* 11 (October 1934): 255-270.

Lowery, Woodbury. *The Spanish Settlements within the Present Limits of the United States, 1513-1574*. 2 vols. New York: Russell and Russell, Inc., 1959.

Ludlum, David M. *Early American Hurricanes, 1492-1870*. Boston: American Meteorological Society, 1963.

McCain, Paul M. *The County Court in North Carolina before 1750*. Durham, N.C.: Duke University Press, 1954.

Merrens, Harry Roy. *Colonial North Carolina in the Eighteenth Century: A Study in Historical Geography*. Chapel Hill: University of North Carolina Press, 1964.

Mobley, Joe A. *James City: A Black Community in North Carolina, 1863-1900*. Raleigh: Division of Archives and History, Department of Cultural Resources, 1981.

_____, ed. *The Way We Lived in North Carolina*. Chapel Hill: University of North Carolina Press, 2003.

Moore, David. "Blackbeard the Pirate: Historical Background and the Beaufort Inlet Shipwrecks." *Tributaries* 7 (1997): 31-36.

Morison, Samuel Eliot. *The European Discovery of America. The Northern Voyages, A.D. 500-1600*. New York: Oxford University Press, 1971.

Parramore, Thomas C. "The Tuscarora Ascendancy." *North Carolina Historical Review* 59 (autumn 1982): 307-326.

Paschal, Herbert R., Jr. *A History of Colonial Bath*. Raleigh: Edwards and Broughton, 1955.

Powell, William S., ed. *Dictionary of North Carolina Biography*. 6 vols. Chapel Hill: University of North Carolina Press, 1979-1996.

_____, ed. *The North Carolina Gazetteer*. Chapel Hill: University of North Carolina Press, 1968.

_____, James K. Huhta, and Thomas J. Farnham, eds. *The Regulators in North Carolina: A Documentary History, 1759-1776*. Raleigh: State Department of Archives and History, 1971.

Price, William S., Jr. " 'Men of Good Estate': Wealth among North Carolina Royal Councillors." *North Carolina Historical Review* 49 (winter 1972): 72-82.

_____. "A Strange Incident in George Burrington's Governorship." *North Carolina Historical Review* 51 (spring 1974): 149-158.

Quinn, David Beers. *North America from Earliest Discovery to First Settlements: The Norse Voyages to 1612*. New York: Harper and Row, 1977.

_____. *Set Fair For Roanoke: Voyages and Colonies, 1584-1606*. Chapel Hill: University of North Carolina Press, 1985.

Rankin, Hugh F. *The Pirates of Colonial North Carolina*. Rev. ed. Raleigh: Division of Archives and History, Department of Cultural Resources, 2001.

Rediker, Marcus. *Between the Devil and the Deep Blue Sea: Merchant Seamen, Pirates, and the Anglo-American Maritime World, 1700-1750*. Cambridge: Cambridge University Press, 1987.

_____. " 'Under the Banner of King Death': The Social World of Anglo-American Pirates, 1716-1726." *William and Mary Quarterly* [3d ser.] 38 (April 1981): 203-227.

Reed, C. Wingate. *Beaufort County: Two Centuries of Its History*. N.p., 1962.

Sandbeck, Peter B. "Dendrochronology: A New Tool for Dating Historic Structures." *Tributaries* 2 (1992): 26-29.

Seventh Biennial Report of the North Carolina Historical Commission. Raleigh: Edwards and Broughton Printing Company, 1919.

Smith, Mary Phlegar. "Borough Representation in North Carolina." *North Carolina Historical Review* 7 (April 1930): 177-191.

Stick, David. *The Outer Banks in North Carolina.* Chapel Hill: University of North Carolina Press, 1958.

"The Tool Bag." *Tributaries* 2 (1992): 31-33.

Towles, Louis P. "Cary's Rebellion and the Emergence of Thomas Pollock." *Journal of the Association of Historians in North Carolina* 4 (fall 1996): 36-58.

Vigneras, L. A. "A Spanish Discovery of North Carolina in 1566." *North Carolina Historical Review* 46 (autumn 1969): 398-414.

Wallace, Wesley H. "North Carolina's Agricultural Journals, 1838-1861." *North Carolina Historical Review* 36 (July 1959): 275-306.

Watson, Alan D. "The Colonial Tavern: A Gathering Place in the Albemarle." In *A Taste of the Past: Foodways of the Albemarle Region, 1585-1830.* Ed. Barbara E. Taylor. Elizabeth City, N.C.: The Museum of the Albemarle, 1991.

_____. "The Committees of Safety and the Coming of the American Revolution in North Carolina, 1774-1776." *North Carolina Historical Review* 73 (April 1996): 131-155.

_____. "The Constable in Colonial North Carolina." *North Carolina Historical Review* 68 (January 1991): 1-16.

_____. "The Ferry in Colonial North Carolina: A Vital Link in Transportation." *North Carolina Historical Review* 51 (summer 1974): 249-266.

_____. *A History of New Bern and Craven County.* New Bern: Tryon Palace Commission, 1987.

_____. "Household Size and Composition in Pre-Revolutionary North Carolina." *Mississippi Quarterly* 31 (fall 1978): 551-569.

_____. "Impulse Toward Independence: Resistance and Rebellion among North Carolina Slaves, 1750-1775." *Journal of Negro History* 63 (fall 1978): 317-328.

_____. "Port Brunswick in the Colonial Era." *Lower Cape Fear Historical Society Journal* 31 (June 1989): 23-34.

_____. "Society and Economy in Colonial Edgecombe County." *North Carolina Historical Review* 50 (summer 1973): 231-255.

_____. *Society in Colonial North Carolina*. Rev. ed. Raleigh: Division of Archives and History, Department of Cultural Resources, 1996.

_____. "The Town Fathers of Early Wilmington, 1743-1775." Lower Cape Fear Historical Society *Bulletin* 24 (October 1980).

Weeks, Stephen B. "Libraries and Literature in North Carolina in the Eighteenth Century." In *Annual Report of the American Historical Association, 1895*. Washington: Government Printing Office, 1896.

Woodson, Carter G., ed. *Free Negro Owners of Slaves in the United States in 1830*. Washington: Association for the Study of Negro Life and History, 1924.

Unpublished

"Address of the Honorable Lindsay C. Warren delivered at Bath, June 19th, 1924, on the occasion of the unveiling of the tablet erected by the State Historical Commission to commemorate the 219th anniversary of the incorporation of the town." Copy on file at Historic Bath State Historic Site, Bath, N.C.

Angley, Wilson. "The Bonner House Vicinity of Bath, North Carolina: Four Hundred Years of Its History." Historical Research Report, Research Branch, Division of Archives and History, Raleigh, February 1979.

_____. "A History of St. Thomas Episcopal Church, Bath, North Carolina." Historical Research Report, Research Branch, Division of Archives and History, Raleigh, February 1981.

_____. "The Life and Work of Edmund H. Harding." Historical Research Report, Research Branch, Division of Archives and History, Raleigh, 1980.

_____. "Port Bath, North Carolina, in the Eighteenth Century: A Compilation of Records." Historical Research Report, Research Branch, Division of Archives and History, Raleigh, August 1981.

"Bath High School[;] Bath Elementary School[;] Timeline." No date. Copy on file at Historic Bath State Historic Site, Bath, N.C.

Boyd, Cottie. Oral interview. Tape recording, August 21, 2003. Historic Bath State Historic Site, Bath, N.C.

Castro, Marilyn Dee. "Historical Houses of Beaufort County, North Carolina, 1744-1899." Ph.D. diss., University of North Carolina at Greensboro, 1982.

Chalker, Nancy, comp. "The History of Bath United Methodist Church, 1892-1992." Ca. 1992. Copy on file at Historic Bath State Historic Site, Bath, N.C.

Cross, Jerry L. "Historical Research Report, Van Der Veer House, Bath, North Carolina." Research Branch, Division of Archives and History, Raleigh, October 1975.

_____. "The Palmer-Marsh House." Historical Research Report, Research Branch, Division of Archives and History, Raleigh, August 1976.

Gibson, John Kenneth. "Thomas Bray Libraries, St. Thomas Parish, Pamlico (Bath, North Carolina), 1700: A Bibliographical and Historical Analysis." Master's thesis, University of North Carolina, 1986.

"History of the Bath Christian Church." No date. Copy on file at Historic Bath State Historic Site, Bath, N.C.

Lawing, Michelle F. "Historical Research Report on Edna Ferber's Visit to Bath, North Carolina." Research Branch, Division of Archives and History, Raleigh, June 1979.

Little, Stanley L. "Bath African Methodist Episcopal Zion Church." Historical Research Report, Division of State Historic Sites, Office of Archives and History, Raleigh, 2003.

Logan, Byron Eugene. "An Historical Geographic Survey of North Carolina Ports." Ph.D. diss., University of North Carolina, 1956.

Lowery, Charles Bryan. "Class, Politics, Rebellion and Regional Development in Proprietary North Carolina (1697-1720)." Ph.D. diss., University of Florida, 1979.

McCartney, Martha W. "History [of] Bath Town, North Carolina." Williamsburg: Virginia Research Center for Archaeology, 1978.

Paschal, Herbert R., Jr. "Proprietary North Carolina: A Study in Colonial Government." Ph.D. diss., University of North Carolina, 1961.

_____. "Tuscarora Indians in North Carolina." Master's thesis, University of North Carolina, 1953.

Styrna, Christine. "The Tuscarora War, 1711-1713: The Struggle for Power, Profit, and Survival." Presented to the American Society of Ethnohistory, Williamsburg, Va., 1988.

Watson, Alan D. "The European Discovery of North Carolina." Presented at the Schiele Museum, Gastonia, N.C., 1984.

Websites

www.ah.dcr.state.nc.us/sections/hp/colonial/editions/Acts/duty.htm

www.ah.dcr.state.nc.us/sections/hp/colonial/editions/Acts/ports.htm

Index

A

Act of Grace, 80, 81
Adams, John, 94
Adams Creek, 5
Adventure (ship), 65
African Americans, 88-90, 102, 112-115
African Methodist Episcopal Zion Church, 116, 128, 129
Albemarle County: Anglican missionaries in, 98; Anglicans in, resent library at Bath, 96-97; effects of Tuscarora War upon, 22; elimination of, 6; inordinate representation of, in General Assembly, 15-16, 43-44; organization of, 4; representation conflict of, with Bath County, 14-16; slow growth of, 5, 8
Albemarle Sound, 52, 53, 75, 78
Aldershire (Aldershair, Aldershare), Mary, 29, 88
Alderson, Simon, 7, 9, 12, 69, 98
Alderson, Simon, Jr., 15
Alexander, William, 54
Algonquian Indians, 2
Amadas, Philip, 2
Angley, Wilson, 97
Anne I, 16
Arcadia, 2
Archbell, Carlton, 118
Archbell, J. B., 119
Archbell Point, 119
Archdale, John, 5, 14-15, 16
Archdale Precinct, 5
Armstrong, Thomas, 69
Arnold, William, Mrs., 118
Aronson, Stuart, 129
Ashe, John Baptista, 55
"Association for the Restoration and Preservation of St. Thomas Episcopal Church, Bath," 122
Aurora, N.C., 114

B

Back Creek, 5, 12, 75
Bailey, Thomas, 97-98

Baptists, 94
Barlowe, Arthur, 2
Barnwell, John, 20-21
Barrow, John, 35, 98
Barrow, William, 7, 15
Bath, N.C.: African Americans in, 88-90, 112-115; Anglican ministers in, 86, 95, 97-102, 113; archaeological excavations at, 13, 84-85; artisans in, 69; bicentennial of founding of, 117, 121; Blackbeard in, 80-82, 126; during Cary's Rebellion, 15-18; celebration of 250th anniversary of, 125-127; centennial of founding of, 117; Charles Eden settles at, 22, 80, 82, 97; churches in, 93-95, 98-102, 104, 112-113, 116-117, 121, 122-124, 127-129; in the Civil War, 113-115; constables in, 36, 38; contested elections in, 42-43; courthouse in, 31, 33-35, 98, 109; customs officials at, 54-56; decline of, 109-110; is designated a port of entry, 22, 52-53; is designated a state historic site, 129; development of, boosted by General Assembly, 28-29; education in, 102-103, 113, 116, 120, 121; effects of Tuscarora War upon, 33, 75, 93; executive council convenes at, 38-39; fence around, 32; ferriages to, 78-79, 103, 110; ferry keepers in, 79; fires in, 118, 129; fishing at, 116; General Assembly convenes at, 38, 40, 44; governance of, 28-32, 36, 38, 120; is granted borough representation, 41; historic preservation movement in, 121-124, 127-129; history of, written, 126; houses in, 84-85, 90-92, 110-112, 115, 125, 127-129; incorporation of, 9, 28; as inspection site, 56; during inter-colonial wars, 44; jail in, 31, 34, 35, 90; library at, 95-97, 98, 100; is located to develop trade through Ocracoke Inlet, 51-52; lumber mills near, 115; merchants in, 7, 14, 68-69, 104, 115, 118; monument to founding of, 121-122; photographer of street scenes in, 119-120; plantations near, 57; postal service at, 103-104; prominent residents

of, 82-83, 86-87; raises company to serve against Regulators, 45; repair of streets in, 33; representatives of, in General Assembly, 42-43; during the Revolutionary War, 45-46, 109-110; roads to, 33, 77-79, 103, 120, 122; Sauthier map of, 32, 35; as seat of county government, 7, 14, 33-36, 104, 109-110; settlement of, 5-7, 9, 12-13, 27, 51, 52; ship owners in, 68-69; shipbuilding and repair at, 65-66, 113; slow growth of, 75-76, 115; survey of, 28; tavern keepers in, 69-71, 91, 92-93; town commissioners of, 28-32, 38, 83, 86, 98, 120; town common in, 32; in the Tuscarora War, 19-22; visit of Edna Ferber to, 124, 127; voting restrictions in, 41-42; women in, 70, 79, 87-88

Bath Christian Church, 116, 127

Bath County: Anglican missionaries in, 98; conflicts of, with Albemarle County, 14-16, 43-44; courts in, 33; creation of, 5; division of, into precincts, 5; economy of, 60; effects of Cary's Rebellion upon, 18; effects of Tuscarora War upon, 19-20, 75; elimination of, 6; library in, 95-96; residents of, petition for port town, 53; settlement of, 6-8, 76-77

Bath County Court of Pleas and Quarter Sessions, 14

Bath Creek: bridge over, 121, 122; early settlers on, 7; gristmills on, 14, 118; Native American settlement on, 5; plantations on, 6, 82; sawmills on, 111, 115; ships anchor in, 14, 85, 126; site for town on, selected by John Lawson, 12; is unsuitable for commerce, 75

Bath Elementary School, 121

Bath High School, 116, 120

Bath Historical Society, 121

Bath Manufacturing Company, 115

Bath Methodist Church, 112, 127

Bath monument, 121-122

Bath Packett (ship), 61

Bath Restoration Committee, 123

Battle of Alamance, 45

Bear Indians, 19

Bear Inlet, 51

Beaufort, N.C.: allotment of constables for, 36; is designated a port of entry, 53; founding of, 27; incorporation of, 53;

lacks marine repair capabilities, 66; municipal government of, 31; occupation of, by Spanish, 44; stagnation of growth of, 76

Beaufort County: contributes company to service against Regulators, 45; county seat of, 34-35, 104, 109; effects of Civil War upon, 114; establishment of, 6; free blacks in, 112-113; inspection sites and public warehouses in, 56; objects to unequal representation, 44; occupation of, by Federal troops, 113; schools in, 102, 116; slaves in, 89, 112-113; women in, 87-88

Beaufort County Agricultural Society, 113

Beaufort County Board of Commissioners, 121

Beaufort County (Precinct) Court of Pleas and Quarter Sessions: appoints ferry keepers, 79; approves rates for taverns, 70-71; composition of, 36; justices of, serve as trustees of library, 96; offices of, in Bath, 104; powers and duties of, 31, 36, 38, 70-71, 79; relocation of, 34-35; responsibilities of, for courthouse and jail, 31

Beaufort County Historical Society, 127-128, 129

Beaufort (Old Topsail) Inlet, 12, 51, 80, 82

Beaufort Precinct, 5-6, 33, 93, 94, 96

Bermuda, 64

Birkenhead, George, 14, 15

Bishir, Catherine, 91

Blackbeard, 80-82, 126, 129

Blackbeard: Knight of the Black Flag, 129

Blackburn, Oliver, 68

Blair, John, 97

Blango, Gabriel, 113

Blinn, Daniel, 31, 68

Blinn, Mourning, 70

Blin(n), Nathaniel, 68, 90

Blinn, Peter, 42, 43, 56, 101-102

Blount, Nathaniel, 102

Blount, Chief Tom, 19

Blount's Creek, 7

Bogue Inlet, 51

Bond, Mrs. _____, 70, 79

Bond, John, 79

Bonner, Caroline, 114

Bonner, Emily, 114

Bonner, James, 35, 109

Bonner, Joseph, 111-112, 113, 114, 116
Bonner, Joseph Y., 116
Bonner, Sallie, 114
Bonner, Thomas, 35, 109, 114
Bonner, Thomas, Jr., 34-35
Bonner, William Vines, 113-114
Bonner House: acquisition and restoration of, by Beaufort County Historical Society, 128-129; construction of, 111-112; occupation of, by Confederate troops, 113; occupation of, by extended Bonner family, 114; pictured, 111; site of, selected by John Lawson, 13; transfer of, to State of North Carolina, 129
Bonner's Point (Town Point), 68, 69, 88, 116, 118
Bonnet, Stede, 80
Borough representation, 41
Boston, Mass., 61
Boston Tea Party, 45
Boutwell, Samuel, 15
Bowdoin, James, 68
Bowen, Charles W., 111, 118
Bowen, Surry, 121
Boyd, Robert, 31, 42
Boyd, Thomas, 55
Bray, Thomas, 94, 95-97
Brazier, R. H. B., 110
Brett, Daniel, 95, 97
Brice, William, 6, 7, 20
Brickell, James, 70
Brickell, John, 10, 75, 94
Brooks, Cicero H., 115
Brooks, Katie, 119
Brooks, Marion, 121
Brooks, Ruth, 119
Brooks, Timothy A., 115, 117, 118, 121
Broughton, Edward, 68
Brown, John, 33, 36, 69
Brown, William, 42, 46, 54, 68, 103-104
Brunswick Town, N.C.: allotment of constables for, 36; Anglican church in, 98, 99; founding of, 27; is granted borough representation, 41; on King's Highway, 77, 103; municipal government of, 31; occupation of, by Spanish, 44; stagnation of growth of, 76
Bunyan, N.C., 121
Burras, John, 7
Burrington, George: assaults Roger Kenyon, 43, 83, 92; declares many

volumes lost from Bath library, 97; governorship of, 43, 54; quoted, 52; recommends Matthew Rowan for executive council, 83
Burroughs, Charles, 92
Byrd, William, 10

C

Caila, Jane, 88
Caila, Peter, 36
Cairnes, Alexander, 68
Calef (Calf), James, 44, 56, 68
Campbell (ship), 63
Campbellton, N.C., 27, 30, 41
Cannon, Uriah, 76-77
Cape Fear, 1, 51
Cape Fear River: failure of early settlement on, 4, 9; port of entry designated for, 54; produces rice and indigo for export, 57; settlement and growth along, 66, 75
Cape Lookout, 51
Capital of North Carolina, 39, 40, 44, 75
Carolina Charter of 1663, 8, 93
Carolina Charter of 1665, 93
Carty, Eleanor, 34
Cary, Thomas, 14, 15-18, 65
Cary's Rebellion, 14-18
Caswell, Richard, 87
Catawba Indians, 20
Catechna (Hancock's Fort), 19, 20, 21
Charles II, 4
Charles Town, N.C., 9
Charleston, S.C., 55, 80
Charlotte, N.C., 27
Charming Polly (ship), 66
Chauncy, Wally, 69
Cherry Point Air Wing Band, 127
Chilly, John, 70
Chowan Precinct, 96
Chowan River, 75
Christian Church, Disciples of Christ, 116
Church of England (Anglican Church): builds churches in North Carolina, 99; concern of Charles Eden for welfare of, 82; is established as official religion, 15, 93-94; ministers of, are active in education, 102; power of taxation objected to, 95; is renamed after American Revolution, 102, 112
Civil War, 112-115

Clarke, John, 68, 88, 94
Clarke, Mary, 88
Clayton, Thomas B., 118
Clements, Giles, 70
Coe, Joffre L., 5
Colleson, John, 69
Collins, Richard, 7
Committees of safety, 46
Concessions and Agreement of 1665, 8, 93
Concorde (ship), 80
Confiscation Acts, 87
Connor, Andrew, 69
Conrow, Jacob, 9
Constables, 36-38
Continental congresses, 45-46
Core Indians, 19, 21
Core Point, 56, 70, 79
Cotan, 2
Cotton, Mary, 88
County courts, 36, 76
Coutanche, Michael: is appointed port
    commissioner, 56; is appointed town
    commissioner of Bath, 31; builds
    Palmer-Marsh House, 84-85, 91-92, 111;
    objects to relocation of county seat, 34;
    is ordered to repair jail, 35; owns
    plantation near Bath, 57; serves in
    colonial assembly, 42; settles in Bath, 61,
    68; sketch of, 86
Coutanche, Sarah, 86
Craven Precinct, 5
Crofton, Henry, 68
Cross Creek, N.C., 27
Culpeper's Rebellion, 14
Currituck Inlet, 1
Currituck Sound, 53
Customs districts, 52-54, 66, 67, 110
Customs officials, 54-55, 56, 82, 110
Cutler, Robert, 68, 69

D

Da Verazzano, Giovanni, 1-2
Daniel, Robert, 7, 15, 16
Darst, Thomas, 122
Davis, James, 100
Daw, Nicholas, 12
De Ayllon, Lucas Vasquez, 1
De Santa Cruz, Alonso, 1
De Villafane, Angel, 1
Dearham, Thomas, 77

Depee, David, 7
Dido (slave), 89
Diocese of East Carolina, 97, 128, 129
Diocese of North Carolina, 112
Dispatch (ship), 60, 69
Dobbs, Arthur, 41, 44, 66, 75-76, 86
Dr. Bray's Associates, 102
Draper, Thomas R., 119, 120
Draper (ship), 65
Draper Building, 118
Drinkwater, John, 28, 94
Duke, William H., 118
Duncan, Abraham, 70
Durham's Creek, 86, 101

E

Earl, Daniel, 102
Eborn, Luther, 113
Eden, Charles: is named to vestry of St.
    Thomas Parish, 94; pardons Blackbeard
    and crew, 80; relationship of, with
    Blackbeard, 80-82; reports threats from
    Indians near Bath, 22; seeks Anglican
    missionary for St. Thomas Parish, 97;
    settles in Bath, 22, 97; sketch of, 82
Eden House (plantation), 82
Edenton, N.C.: is accorded borough
    representation, 41; allotment of commis-
    sioners for, 30; allotment of constables
    for, 36; Anglican church built at, 98-99;
    courthouse constructed at, 34; is desig-
    nated a port of entry, 53; fence around,
    32; ferry crossing to, 78; founding of, 27;
    growth of, overshadows Bath, 75-76; on
    King's Highway, 77, 103; is offered
    library by Edward Moseley, 97; receives
    cannon from Bath, 109; school opens
    near, 102; serves as colonial capital, 39,
    44; voting restrictions in, 41-42
Elizabeth I, 2
Elizabeth (ship), 60, 66
Elizabeth and Ann (ship), 44
Elliott Brothers, 118
Episcopalians, 112, 122
Executive council, 38, 39, 40, 83, 86
*Explication to the Catechism of the Church of
    England, An*, 97
Exports, 56-61

F

Farmer's Journal, 113
Farrow Shipyard, 125
Fences, 32
Ferber, Edna, 125, 127
Ferries, 78-79, 103, 110
Ferry keepers, 78, 79
Finlay, Hugh, 79, 103-104
First Continental Congress, 46
Fletcher, Inglis, 127
Fort Granville, 56
Fort Nohoroco (Neoheroka, Nookerooka), 21
Fox, George, 93
Frazier, Andrew, 93
Free blacks, 112-113
Freedmen's Bureau Bank, 114, 115
Freeman, John, 79
French and Indian War, 44
Friendship (ship), 69
Fundamental Constitutions of 1669, 8, 88, 93

G

Gale, Christopher: erects gristmill on Bath Creek, 14; forfeits lot in Bath, 28; hosts church services, 94; is named to vestry of St. Thomas Parish, 94; portrait of, 83; provides temporary home for Bath library, 96; site of former home of, hosts 250th anniversary events, 127; sketch of, 82
Gale, Miles, 82, 94
Gale, Thomas, 96
Gale, William, 95
Garganus, Francis, 7
Garzia, John, 29, 98, 99, 100
Garzia, Mary, 100
General Assembly: appoints commissioners for Bath, 28, 30-31; appoints commissioners for Port Bath, 55-56; asserts power against executive branch, 22; authorizes erection of fences around towns, 32; charters towns with borough representation, 41; codifies and revises laws, 22, 28; composition of, 39; confirms incorporation of Bath, 28, 30; considers Bath for provincial capital, 75; control of, by Hyde faction, 16; creates Historic Bath Commission, 128; decides contested elections, 42-43; designates Bath a state historic site, 129; eliminates Albemarle and Bath Counties, 6; encourages urbanization, 8; enlarges boundaries of Bath, 120; erects Pitt County, 35; establishes Church of England as official religion, 15; establishes inspection system for exports, 56; establishes municipal governments, 29-31; incorporates Washington, 109; inequality of representation in, 15-16, 43-44; levies tariff on imports, 64; meets at Bath, 38, 40, 44; notes decrease of trade at Port Bath, 66; orders appointment of keeper for Bath-Core Point ferry, 79; orders construction of courthouse and jail in Bath, 33, 34, 35; orders relocation of Beaufort County courthouse, 34-35; passes new vestry act, 94; provides for care of library at Bath, 96-97; provides for construction of Anglican church at Bath, 98; recognizes St. Thomas Parish, 94; recognizes town common in Bath, 32; relieves townsmen from working on county roads, 33; representatives from Bath in, 42, 83, 86; requires construction of houses to retain ownership of lots, 28; requires licensing of taverns, 93; restricts building along waterfront, 29; restricts gaming in taverns, 71; transforms precincts into counties, 6
General Court, 36, 82
George II, 39
Georgetown, S.C., 77, 103
Gibbs, John, 14
Gibbs's Rebellion, 14
Glebe land and house, 86, 100-101, 127
Glover, William, 15, 16
Goodwill (ship), 60
Gordon, Patrick, 42, 43
Gordon, William, 13, 97
Gould, George, 54
Gould (Gold), Stephen, 55
Graffenried, Baron Christoph von, 19, 27
Granville, John (Earl of Bath), 5
Great Alligator Dismal Swamp, 78
Great Awakening, 99
Great Britain, 61-63, 65
Grenville, Sir Richard, 2
Greyhound (ship), 60
Griffin, Charles, 102

H

Haag, William G., 5
Halifax, N.C., 27, 41, 109, 110
Hamilton, Alexander, 29
Hamilton, B. F., 118
Hancock, Chief, 19
Handy's Point, 5
Harding, Edmund Hoyt, 127, 128
Harding, Israel, 112, 113
Harding, Thomas: agrees to build ship for
    Thomas Cary, 14, 65; is appointed
    commissioner of Bath, 28; is appointed to
    vestry of St. Thomas Parish, 94; builds
    ships, 65, 69; owns plantation near Bath, 57
Hardy, Grizle, 79
Hargott, Frederick, 34
Hatteras Indians, 19
Hazard, Ebenezer, 78, 104-105
Heath, Sir Robert, 4
Hertford, N.C., 27
Hillsborough, N.C., 27, 41
Hilton, H. G., 114
Historic Bath Commission, 127-128, 129
Historic Bath State Historic Site, 127-128,
    129
Hitty (ship), 60
Hodges, Luther H., 127
Hogg, James, 76
Homann, J. B., 22
Hornigold, Benjamin, 80
House of Commons, 39, 40, 41
Howcott (Houit, Howcut), Edward, 57, 70,
    90, 91
Huguenots, 7-8, 12, 93
Hyde, Edward, 16-18, 21
Hyde Precinct, 5, 33

I

Indian Island, 5
Inlets, 51-52
Innes, James, 102
Intolerable Acts, 45
Inventories of estates, 76-77

J

Jack (slave), 90
Jackson Swamp, 111, 113, 115
Jadrian, _____, 12

James Adams Floating Theatre, 125
James City, N.C., 113, 114, 115
Jewell, Thomas, 98
Johnston, Gabriel: convenes executive
    council at Bath, 39; convenes General
    Assembly at Bath, 40; convenes General
    Assembly to hear representation
    controversy, 44; governorship of, 43;
    intercedes on behalf of John Garzia, 98;
    lodges in tavern at Bath, 70; niece of,
    marries Alexander Stewart, 86; quoted, 8-9
Johnston, Penelope, 86
Johnston, Samuel, 86
Jones, Adam, 36
Jones, Nicholas, 89
Jones, Richard, 69
Jones, Thomas Nicholas, 7
Jones, William, 68
Jordan, John, 14
Junior Order United American Mechanics,
    118

K

Keais, Nathan, 54, 110
Keel, Bennie C., 5
Kenyon, Roger: is assaulted by George
    Burrington, 43, 83, 92; court actions
    involving, 92-93; operates tavern in Bath,
    70, 93; owns plantation near Bath, 57;
    property of, is stolen, 88; prospers after
    settling in Bath, 68; represents Bath in
    colonial assembly, 42-43; sketch of,
    82-83
King George's War, 44
King's Highway, 77, 103
Kinston, N.C., 27
Kirby Grange, 127
Kitty Hawk, N.C., 1-2
Knight, Tobias, 80, 81, 94

L

Lane, Ralph, 2
Larke (Lark), Thomas, 69, 88
Latham, William, 110
Lawson, Isabella, 13, 88
Lawson, John: admires Native Americans,
    10-11; is appointed commissioner to
    survey boundary with Virginia, 10; buys
    land from David Perkins, 9; claims Town

Point, 68; daughter of, receives property of, 13, 88; death of, 19; defenses erected on property of, 19-20; erects gristmill on Bath Creek, 14; former property of, purchased, 88, 91, 111; leaves property to daughter and Hannah Smith, 13; quoted, 57-58, 58-59; selects site for Bath, 12; selects site for New Bern, 27; settles along Bath Creek, 7, 12-13, 68; sketch of, 9-10, 12; surveys interior of Carolina, 9; underestimates strength of Tuscarora, 18
Leahy (Lakey), John, 42
Lewis, George, 34
Library at Bath, 95-97, 98, 100
Lillington, John, 19, 94
Livestock, 32, 57
Logan, William, 69, 75, 79, 90
Lords Proprietors of Carolina: actions of, during Cary's Rebellion, 15-18; appoint commissioners to survey boundary with Virginia, 10; appoint John Lawson to survey interior, 9; are granted Carolina by Charles II, 4; promote settlement by encouraging urbanization, 6, 8, 28; promote settlement through religious tolerance, 93; return colony to Crown, 43; sanction slavery in colony, 88
Lost Colony, The, 127
Low, Emanuell, 15, 17, 18
Low, Nevil, 15
Loyalist Claims Commission, 87
Ludwell, Philip, 14
Luellyn, Maurice, 12, 14
Lumber mills, 115

M

McCulloh, Henry, 39
McDonagh, Michael, 29, 69
McMahon, Bryan, 69
Mace, William, 68
Machapunga Indians, 19, 21
Manakin Town (Manokin, Mannakintown), Va., 7-8
Marion (boat), 118, 119
Marsh, David, 114
Marsh, G. W., 119
Marsh, Jonathan, 111
Marsh Store, 118

Martin, Joel, 7, 9, 12, 28
Martinsborough, N.C., 31
Mary (ship), 60
Mary and Betsey (ship), 68
Mason, Maud, 119
Mason, William W., 118
Mattson, John L., 5
Maule, John, 42, 89
Maule, Patrick, 55, 94
Maynard, Robert, 81
Merrick (slave), 90
Methodists, 112
Metropolitan African Methodist Episcopal Zion Church, 116
Midgette, William B., 127
Ming, Joseph, 89
Mitchell, William, 69
Modern Woodmen of the World, 118
Moir, James, 102
Molasses Act, 55
Molly (ship), 44
Moore, James, 21
Moore, Maurice, 55, 81
Moore, Richard, 34
Morgan, Joseph, 29
Moseley, Edward, 10, 16, 81, 97
Movil (Moville) Trader, 82
Municipal governments in North Carolina, 29-33, 38
Murray, James, 40

N

Naval, Robert, 68-69
Naval stores, 58-59
Navigation Acts, 52, 54
Neuse River, 53-54, 75, 78
Neusioc Indians, 19
Neverson Quarry, 121
Nevill, James, 7
New Bern, N.C.: is abandoned during Tuscarora War, 22; allotment of constables for, 36; citizens of, authorized to elect town commissioners, 31; control of livestock in, 32; is designated capital of colony, 39, 44, 75; falls to Federal troops, 113; is granted borough representation, 41; growth of, eclipses Bath, 75, 76; Huguenots settle in, 8; John Lawson builds house at site of, 10, 27;

newspapers published at, 103; is placed
in Port Beaufort customs district, 53-54;
roads to, 77, 78-79, 103, 110; settlement
of, triggers Tuscarora War, 19
New Bern (ship), 68
New Currituck Inlet, 51
New Inlet, 51
New River Inlet, 51
New Voyage to Carolina, A, 10, 12
Newburn (ship), 63
Newman, Thomas, 97-98
Newspapers, 103
Nicholson, Dr. _____, 118
Nicholson, Francis, 18
Nixonton, N.C., 27, 102
"Noble Savage," 10, 12
Noe, Alexander Constantine Davis, 123,
124, 128
Norfolk-Southern Railroad, 121
North Carolina Department of Cultural
Resources, 129
North Carolina Historical Commission, 121
North Carolina Office of Archives and
History, 129

O

Ocracoke Inlet: African American pilots at,
89; Blackbeard killed at, 81; is blockaded
by Royal Navy, 109-110; commercial
importance of, 51-52; distance of, from
Bath, 12; levy collected to mark channels
in, 55-56
Odeon, Charles, 98
Odeon, John, 98
Old Currituck Inlet, 51
Old Town Creek, 5, 6, 7
Opuscula Mythologica, Ethica et Physica, 96
Ormond, Henry, 125
Ormond, Roger, 46, 54
Ormond, Wyriot, 35, 42, 43, 56, 69
Ormond, Wyriot, Jr., 42, 43, 103
Oscar F. Smith Memorial Foundation, 128
Ottiwell, Isaac, 54
Outer Banks, 1-2, 43, 51-52, 109-110
Owen, Thomas, 69
Owen, William, 54

P

Palmer, Margaret, 87
Palmer, Robert: is appointed commissioner
for construction of courthouse, 35; as
member of executive council, 39; objects
to relocation of county seat, 34; as owner
of Palmer-Marsh House, 92, 110-111;
owns plantation near Bath, 57; portrait
of, 88; represents Bath in colonial
assembly, 42; serves against Regulators,
45; serves as commissioner of navigation
and pilotage, 56; serves as customs
collector, 54; serves as entry taker, 104;
sketch of, 86-87; as slaveholder, 89
Palmer, William, 54, 68-69, 87, 92, 111
Palmer-Marsh House: is acquired and
restored by Beaufort County Historical
Society, 128; advertisement for sale of,
92; archaeological excavations in vicinity
of, 84-85; as boardinghouse, 125; church
built behind, 112; construction of, 84,
86; is damaged by fire, 129; description
of, 91; Edna Ferber visits, 125; passes to
Marsh family, 110-111, 114; pictured, 91;
is purchased by Robert Palmer, 86, 92; is
transferred to State of North Carolina, 129
Pamlico Indians, 2, 5, 19
Pamlico River: distance of Bath from
mouth of, 52; ferriages across, 76, 78-79;
Native American settlements along, 4; is
unsuited for commerce, 75; Washington
secures trade on, 109
Pamlico Sound, 2, 52, 53
Pamptecough Precinct, 5, 8, 96
Pamtecough (Pamticoe), 5
Pantego Creek, 114
Parliament, 45, 58
Parsons, Samuel, 68
Paschal, Herbert, 126
Patten (Patton), John, 45
Peco, Daniel, 69
Peggy Tryon (ship), 63
Pendergrass, Margaret, 88
Perdree, _____, 12
Periaugers, 65, 66
Perkins, David, 7, 9, 12
Perquimans Precinct, 9
Peter (Indian), 89
Petway, Diane, 127
Peyton, Benjamin, 31

Phillips, Catherine, 90, 93
Pitt County, 35
Pollock, Thomas, 15, 16, 17, 20, 21
Polly (ship), 60
Pomoik Indians, 2
Port Bath: Bath designated port of entry
    for, 52-53; commissioners of, 55-56;
    customs collectors of, 39, 46, 54, 86, 110;
    decline of, 66-67; discontinuance of, 110;
    establishment of, 53; exports from, 57,
    59-61; imports to, 62-64; volume of
    trade at, 55, 59-67
Port Beaufort, 53, 59, 66, 67, 82
Port Brunswick, 53-55, 59, 60, 64-65, 67
Port Currituck, 53, 59, 65-67, 82
Port Roanoke, 53, 59, 66-67, 82
Port Washington, 110
Porter, Edmund, 15, 18
Porter, Edward, 68
Porter, John, 15, 18, 28, 55, 94
Postmasters, 103-104
Potter, Robert, 69
Powhatan Indians, 2
Presbyterians, 93-94
Privy Council, 17, 39
Protestant Episcopal Church, 102, 112
Providence (ship), 63

Q

Quakers (Society of Friends), 14-15, 18, 90
Quary, Robert, 7
Queen Anne's Bell, 127
Queen Anne's Revenge (ship), 80, 82
Queen Anne's War, 19, 44, 80
Quincy, Josiah, Jr., 87
Quinn, David Beers, 4
Quitrents, 43

R

Rainsford, Giles, 96, 97
Raleigh, Sir Walter, 2
Ranger (ship), 60
Ravenscroft, John Starke, 112
Red Banks, 56
Reed, C. Wingate, 15
Regulator movement, 45, 86
Representation controversy, 43-44
Respess, Thomas, 35, 43, 56, 90
Revolutionary War, 109-110

Rice, Nathaniel, 83
Richardson, Daniel, 94
Rieusset, _____, 90
Rieusset, John, 31, 54, 57
Rigby, Richard, 42, 69
Rigby, William, 68
Roach, _____, 16, 17
Roanoke Inlet, 51, 52
Roanoke Island, 2, 9
Roanoke Lumber Company, 115
Robbins, James, 70
Rodman, Lida T., 117, 121
Rodman, William B., 127
Roman Catholics, 94
Roper, Thomas, 69
Roper Lumber Company, 115
Rowan, Matthew, 68, 83, 92-93
Royal Navy, 81, 109-110

S

Salem, N.C., 27
Salisbury, N.C., 27, 30, 31, 41
Sally (ship), 63, 69
Salter, Edward, 34, 98
Sauthier, Claude J., 32
Sauthier maps, 32, 35, 85, 91
Schoepf, Johann, 78
Scott, William, 69
Sea Flower (ship), 60
Second Continental Congress, 46
Secotan, 2, 4
Secotan Indians, 2, 5
Shipbuilding, 65-66, 113, 125
Show Boat, 125
Shute, Giles, 12
Sigley, William, 29
Simmons, Matilda, 114-115
Simpson, _____, 90
Sinclare, Samuel, 56
Singleton, James, 98
Slaves, 88-90, 112-113, 114, 115
Smith, Hannah, 13
Smith, Mary, 70
Smith, Richard, 13
Smith, Ruth Bowen, 129
Society for Promoting Christian
    Knowledge, 95
Society for the Propagation of the Gospel,
    86, 94-95, 97, 98, 100
Sothel, Seth, 5, 9, 14

Spain, 1, 44
Sparrow, Thomas, 15
Speedwill (ship), 60, 61
Spotswood, Alexander, 15, 17, 81
St. Paul's Church, 98, 99
St. Paul's Parish, 96, 102
St. Philips Church, 98
St. Thomas Episcopal Church: is built in center of street, 35, 98; burials at, 87, 124; is cared for by Diocese of East Carolina, 128-129; construction of, 98-99; in the early nineteenth century, 112; glebe set aside for, 86, 100-101; holds special service during 250th anniversary, 127; ministers of, 98-102, 112, 113, 116, 122-124; pictured, 101, 124; repairs to, 100, 112; restoration of, 122-124, 128
St. Thomas Parish: glebe house of, 86; library for, 95-97; ministers of, 98-102; is recognized by Vestry Act, 94; vestrymen of, 83, 94; is visited by Anglican missionaries, 98
Stamp Act, 45
Stephen (slave), 90
Stephens, Richard N., 104
Stewart, Alexander, 86, 89, 100, 101, 102
Stone, Margaret, 82
Stubbs, William, 70
Success (ship), 68
Suffolk, Va., 77, 103
Sugar Act, 55
Swash, The, 55
Swindell, Jack, 117
Swindell's Cash Store, 117

T

T. A. Brooks Grocery, 117, 118
Tankard, Edgar, Mrs., 118
Tankard, Mary Arcadia, 121, 122
Tankard, Thad, 118
Tarboro, N.C., 27, 110
Tarkington, Richard, 118
Tavern keepers, 69-71, 83, 90, 91, 93
Taverns, 69-71, 79, 93, 104
Taylor, Samuel, 70
Tea Act, 45
Teach (Tach, Thach, Tatch), Edward, 80
Thistleworth (plantation), 82
Thomson, Samuel, 69

Tillett, William, 18
Tompkins, John M., 113
Tomson, William, 7
Traverse, Edward, 69
Treasury Board, 54
Trent River, 75
Trimble, John, 68
Truewhite, Levi, 7, 15
Tryon, William, 45, 64, 86-87, 101-102, 103
Tryon Palace, 64
Turner, Robert, 42, 98
Tuscarora Indians, 10, 18-22
Tuscarora War: account of, 18-22; effects of, 22, 27, 33, 75, 93; failure of Virginia to send aid during, 20, 81; Huguenots in Bath are victims of, 93
Tyer, James, Mrs., 118

U

Unday, Thomas, 70
Unity (ship), 61
Urbanization, 6, 8-9, 27-28, 51, 75-76
Urmstone, John, 13, 22, 82, 96, 97-98

V

Validity of Infant Baptism, 100
Van Der Veer, Jacob, 111
Van Der Veer House, 110, 111, 129
Vaughn, William, 68
Virgin (ship), 63, 64
Virginity (ship), 65

W

Walker, Henderson, 15
War of Jenkins' Ear, 44
Ward, Collingwood, 7
Warehouses, 56
Warren, Henry, 15
Warren, Lindsay C., 122, 127
Washington, N.C.: Beaufort County courthouse moved to future site of, 34; is designated a port of entry, 110; is designated county seat of Beaufort County, 35, 109; fish shipped from Bath to, 116; founding of, 109; growth of, eclipses Bath, 110, 112; newspaper at, notes developments in Bath, 115; occupation of, by Federal troops, 113;

religious groups from, visit Bath, 117; sends equipment to fight fire in Bath, 118
Waters, Helen, 121, 122
Watson, Elkanah, 78, 87
Watson, John, 68
Waynick, Capus, 128
Weeks, Stephen B., 97
West Indies, 60-64
White, John, 2
Whitefield, George, 78, 99, 100
Whitmore, Ephraim, 111
Wickham Precinct, 5
Willcocks, James, 102
Williams, Thomas, 69
Willis, Ephraim, 113
Willis, William, 98
Wills, 77-78
Wilmington, N.C.: allotment of constables for, 36; Anglican church built at, 99; citizens of, permitted to nominate town commissioners, 31; control of livestock in, 32; courthouse at, raised on pillars, 31; founding of, 27; is granted borough representation, 41; growth of, 76; on King's Highway, 77, 103; newspapers published in, 103; as seat of provincial government, 39, 44
Windsor, N.C., 27
Winfield, W. O., 118
Winwright, James, 102
Wood products, 57-59
Woodstock, N.C., 31
Woolard, J. S., 119
Worsley, Thomas, 94
Wortham, George W., 113-114
Wyersdale, Nathaniel, 9, 12

Y

Yamasee Indians, 20